VEGETARIAN
COOKING FOR SPECIAL OCCASIONS

VEGETARIAN
COOKING FOR SPECIAL OCCASIONS

MORE THAN 140 IMAGINATIVE RECIPES SHOWN STEP
BY STEP WITH OVER 170 STUNNING PHOTOGRAPHS

VALERIE FERGUSON

southwater

This edition is published by Southwater, an imprint of Anness Publishing Ltd, Hermes House, 88–89 Blackfriars Road, London SE1 8HA; tel. 020 7401 2077; fax 020 7633 9499

www.southwaterbooks.com; www.annesspublishing.com

If you like the images in this book and would like to investigate using them for publishing, promotions or advertising, please visit our website www.practicalpictures.com for more information.

UK distributor: Book Trade Services; tel. 0116 2759086; fax 0116 2759090; uksales@booktradeservices.com; exportsales@booktradeservices.com
North American distributor: National Book Network; tel. 301 459 3366; fax 301 429 5746; www.nbnbooks.com
Australian distributor: Pan Macmillan Australia; tel. 1300 135 113; fax 1300 135 103; customer.service@macmillan.com.au
New Zealand distributor: David Bateman Ltd; tel. (09) 415 7664; fax (09) 415 8892

Publisher: Joanna Lorenz
Editorial Director: Helen Sudell
Editor: Valerie Ferguson
Recipes contributed by: Catherine Atkinson, Alex Barker, Michelle Berriedale-Johnson, Angela Boggiano, Kathy Brown, Carla Capalbo, Kit Chan, Jacqueline Clark, Carole Clements, Trish Davies, Roz Denny, Patrizia Diemling, Matthew Drennan, Sarah Edmonds, Rafi Fernandez, Christine France, Silvana Franco, Shirley Gill, Nicola Graimes, Rosamund Grant, Carole Handslip, Rebekah Hassan, Deh-Ta Hsuing, Shehzad Husain, Christine Ingram, Judy Jackson, Manisha Kanani, Soheila Kimberley, Sara Lewis, Patricia Lousada, Lesley Mackley, Sue Maggs, Kathy Man, Sally Mansfield, Norma Miller, Sallie Morris, Annie Nichols, Maggie Pannell, Katherine Richmond, Jennie Shapter, Anne Sheasby, Liz Trigg, Hilaire Walden, Laura Washburn, Steven Wheeler, Elizabeth Wolf-Cohen and Jeni Wright
Photographers: William Adams-Lingwood, Karl Adamson, Edward Allwright, Steve Baxter, Nicki Dowey, James Duncan, John Freeman, Ian Garlick, Michelle Garrett, John Heseltine, Amanda Heywood, Ferguson Hill, Janine Hosegood, David Jordan, Dave King, Don Last, Patrick McLeavey, Michael Michaels, Steve Moss, Thomas Odulate, Simon Smith, Sam Stowell and Polly Wreford
Designer: Carole Perks
Typesetter: Diane Pullen
Editorial Reader: Linda Doeser
Production Controller: Claire Rae

ETHICAL TRADING POLICY

Because of our ongoing ecological investment programme, you, as our customer, can have the pleasure and reassurance of knowing that a tree is being cultivated on your behalf to naturally replace the materials used to make the book you are holding. For further information about this scheme, go to www.annesspublishing.com/trees

Previously published as *Special Occasion Vegetarian*

NOTES

Bracketed terms are intended for American readers.
For all recipes, quantities are given in both metric and imperial measures and, where appropriate, in standard cups and spoons.
Follow one set of measures, but not a mixture, because they are not interchangeable.
Standard spoon and cup measures are level. 1 tsp = 5ml, 1 tbsp = 15ml, 1 cup = 250ml/8fl oz.
Australian standard tablespoons are 20ml. Australian readers should use 3 tsp in place of 1 tbsp for measuring small quantities.
American pints are 16fl oz/2 cups. American readers should use 20fl oz/2.5 cups in place of 1 pint when measuring liquids.
Electric oven temperatures in this book are for conventional ovens. When using a fan oven, the temperature will probably need to be reduced by about 10–20°C/20–40°F. Since ovens vary, you should check with your manufacturer's instruction book for guidance.
Medium (US large) eggs are used unless otherwise stated.

Main front cover image shows Barley Risotto with Roasted Squash & Leeks – for recipe, see page 52.

PUBLISHER'S NOTE

Although the advice and information in this book are believed to be accurate and true at the time of going to press, neither the authors nor the publisher can accept any legal responsibility or liability for any errors or omissions that may have been made nor for any inaccuracies nor for any loss, harm or injury that comes about from following instructions or advice in this book.

Contents

Introduction

There are many reasons for cooking a special meal, whether you are celebrating a birthday with the family, throwing a party for a number of friends or hoping to impress someone important with a formal dinner. While immensely pleasurable, preparing special occasion dishes

can be quite stressful, especially if you are catering for meat eaters as well as fellow vegetarians. This superb collection of recipes takes the worry out of planning and the hassle out of cooking, so that you, too, can enjoy a memorable meal. Perhaps not by chance, it also demonstrates the versatility, breadth and appeal of vegetarian cooking.

A useful introductory section offers some helpful hints and tips on techniques and gourmet ingredients. It also includes some basic recipes that will make sure your meal has a final professional touch. The recipes themselves are divided into six chapters, making it easy to select complementary courses and choose the style of meal that suits the occasion, whether an elegant riverside picnic on a summer's evening, a family lunch on the patio or a sophisticated dinner party.

Elegant Soups & Appetizers provides a tempting selection of dishes designed to stimulate the appetite in every way – they look, smell and taste simply wonderful. Whether you choose a warming, spicy soup, a beautiful layered terrine or melt-in-the-mouth tartlets, you will be starting your special occasion meal in style.

Party Pieces, Picnics, Brunches & Light Lunches is the chapter to refer to for informal celebrations and larger gatherings. There are tasty, bitesize morsels to serve with drinks, spectacular dishes to grace any buffet table and easily transportable food, such as panini and

delectable pâtés that are just fabulous. There are also more substantial dishes for brunch, lunch or even a special occasion breakfast on New Year's Day or a birthday morning.

Pasta, Pizza & Grains offers exciting twists on familiar themes with innovative recipes for these staples. This is a good place to look if you are cooking for a range of ages, as these dishes appeal to adults and children alike. Many of them are easy on the purse too, proving that you don't have to buy the most expensive ingredients to make a meal special.

Stuffed Vegetables, Baked Dishes, Crêpes & Pastry Dishes provides you with the opportunity to push the boat out. This chapter is packed with recipes for gourmet vegetarian dining, from strudels to gougères and from flans to crêpes. However, you may be pleasantly surprised to discover that many of these superb main course dishes are astonishingly easy to cook.

Side Dishes & Salads features fabulous accompaniments that give any meal the extra touch that makes it truly special. It also includes some sophisticated main course salads that your guests will remember long after the summer sunshine has faded.

The final chapter, Irresistible Bread & Savoury Baking, covers those little extras that distinguish

the perfect host or hostess. Mouthwatering rustic breads, intricate braided loaves, charming little dinner rolls and freshly baked scones (biscuits), while not essential, add an extra dimension to the meal.

Of course, you don't have to wait for a special occasion to try these gourmet delights. If you cook them on any ordinary day, you will turn it into a special one.

Gourmet Vegetarian Ingredients

The cardinal rule when shopping for vegetarian ingredients is to choose the freshest possible produce, buying little and often. For dried goods, find a supplier with a fast turnover, so stocks don't have time to get stale. Keep a constant lookout for new and exciting products. Vegetarian food is a growth market, and the range of available foods is constantly increasing. Once the preserve of the health food store, vegetarian ingredients are now stocked in every supermarket, and the demand for organic produce, and products made from organic ingredients, is huge.

Vegetables

As vegetables lie at the core of the vegetarian diet, it is important to buy the best quality available when it is in peak condition. Ideally make the most of seasonal, local produce. Sun-ripened tomatoes, for example, are invariably sweeter and more flavoursome than those ripened under glass, however beguilingly red. The asparagus of early summer is always more delicately flavoured and has a much better texture than out-of-season imports. You don't have to buy unfamiliar or exotic vegetables to create a gourmet meal, but if you see something you have never tried before, such as okra, kohlrabi, sweet potatoes or one of the many varieties of wild mushrooms now available, be adventurous and, at the same time, extend your repertoire. You should, of course, also be selective when you are buying more familiar vegetables. Supermarkets now provide far more information about their stock and this can be extremely helpful when looking for specific ingredients.

tomatoes

dried and fresh ceps

sweet potatoes

asparagus

Herbs & Spices

The most satisfying way to obtain herbs is from your own garden. You don't need acres of space, as even a window-box or a few pots on the patio will yield a generous harvest. Obvious varieties to grow are mint and parsley, preferably the flat leaf variety, as well as thyme, basil, sage, and oregano or marjoram. If you have space, coriander (cilantro), chives, chervil, tarragon, rosemary and bay are good additions to the herb plot, and all of them feature in this book. Alternatively, buy herbs from the supermarket, but use them as soon as possible after purchase. Dried herbs lose their potency quite quickly, so buy small amounts at a time, keep them in a cool, dry place (out of direct sunlight) and replace them as soon as they start to go stale.

For the best flavour, buy whole spices and seeds, and grind them as needed in a spice mill or coffee grinder kept for the purpose. Dry-frying spices before grinding intensifies their flavour. Essential spices include cardamom pods, cumin and coriander seeds, cinnamon sticks, nutmeg, dried chillies and chilli powder, cayenne, paprika, Chinese five-spice powder, garam masala, saffron, turmeric and curry powder.

basil

flat leaf parsley

cinnamon

chives and bay leaves

coriander seeds and coriander (cilantro) leaves

Clockwise from top: celery seeds, chilli powder, chilli flakes and cayenne

Grains, Pasta & Pulses

Rice is invaluable to the vegetarian cook, both as a base for vegetable stews and sautés and for stuffed vegetables. Try basmati, which has a wonderful fragrance and flavour and is known as the king of rices. Rinse it well before use and, if there is time, soak it in the water used for the final rinse. For risotto, a short grain risotto rice, such as arborio, carnaroli or Vialone Nano is essential. This type of rice can absorb a much larger quantity of liquid than long grain rice so that it acquires a wonderful creamy texture.

Bulgur wheat has already been partially

arborio, carnaroli and Vialone Nano risotto rice

dried pasta

lentils

prepared, so needs only a brief soaking before use. It is ideal for pilaffs and baked dishes.

Dried pasta comes in an astonishing array of shapes and colours and is a good store cupboard standby. An Italian brand is likely to have a reliably good flavour. If you have access to a good Italian delicatessen, it is worth buying fresh pasta. Best of all, make your own pasta dough, using our basic recipe.

dried beans

Pulses, such as dried beans, and the familiar red, green and brown lentils, keep well and play a vital role in vegetarian cooking. Most pulses need to be soaked overnight, so remember to take the time into account when you are planning your special occasion menu. Puy lentils are considered to have the best flavour of all and they retain their soft yet solid texture when cooked.

From the Refrigerator & Freezer

Look for vegetarian versions of your favourite cheeses (produced with vegetable rennet). Always grate cheese freshly, especially Parmesan, rather than buying ready grated, which quickly loses its flavour. When buying mozzarella, look for cheese made from water buffalo's, rather than cow's milk for an authentic flavour. The best mozzarella

mozzarella cheese

sour cream and crème fraîche

comes from Italy and Bulgaria. Yogurt, cream, sour cream, crème fraîche and smetana can add an incomparable richness to sauces.

tofu

Tofu, made from soya beans and a good protein food for vegans, tastes bland but absorbs other flavours well, and can be soft or firm in texture. Tempeh is similar to tofu, but has a nuttier, more pronounced taste. While shortcrust pastry is relatively easy to make, it is worth buying in filo and puff pastry.

From the Larder

In addition to pasta, pulses and grains, you need to keep a stock of other dry goods, such as several types of flour, easy-blend (rapid-rise) dried yeast, polenta and oatmeal and a supply of nuts. Don't buy larder supplies in bulk, as they date if stored for too long.

mixed nuts

Dried mushrooms are invaluable. Porcini, also known as ceps, are the most widely available dried mushrooms, but there are other varieties, including packs of mixed mushrooms. A small quantity added to a dish imparts a wonderfully concentrated flavour.

Other useful items include sun-dried tomatoes, either in packets or packed in oil in jars. The former must be soaked in water before use. Also in jars, look for pesto (both green and red), tahini, peanut butter, capers and olives. Useful sauces include passata (bottled strained tomatoes), creamed horseradish, soy sauce and the vegetarian version of Worcestershire sauce. You'll need various vinegars, including balsamic. While expensive, it has a unique, mellow flavour. A bland tasting oil, such as sunflower, is perfect for general cooking, but there are recipes when only olive oil will do – and then it should be the highest quality extra virgin. This, too, is expensive, but there is no substitute.

balsamic vinegar

extra virgin olive oil

Techniques

Even the simplest tasks in the kitchen can take longer than necessary if you don't know a few useful techniques and short cuts. Below are some step-by-step instructions for preparing a variety of ingredients that will save time and help to improve the presentation of the final dishes. No special equipment is required for most of them, just a sharp knife.

Chopping Onions

1 Cut a peeled onion in half lengthways and place one half, cut side down, on a board. Slice it vertically several times.

2 Make two horizontal cuts in from the stalk end towards the root, but not through it. Holding the onion by the root end, cut it crossways to form even diced pieces.

Cutting Vegetable Batons

1 Peel firm vegetables and cut in 5cm/2in lengths. Cut these into 3mm/⅛in slices.

2 Stack the slices and cut them neatly lengthways into thin batons.

Peeling & Chopping Tomatoes

1 Cut a cross in the blossom end of each tomato. Put them in a heatproof bowl and pour over boiling water.

2 Leave for 30 seconds, until the skins wrinkle and start to peel back from the crosses. Drain, peel off the skins and chop the flesh neatly.

Chopping Herbs

1 Remove any thick stalks and discard. Pile the herbs on a board and chop them finely, first in one direction, then the other, using a sharp knife or a mezzaluna (half-moon herb chopper), which you use in a see-saw motion.

Blanching Vegetables

1 Bring a pan of water to the boil. Using a wire basket, if possible, lower the vegetables into the water and bring it back to the boil.

2 Cook for 1–2 minutes, then drain the vegetables and cool them quickly under cold running water or by dipping them in a bowl of iced water. Drain well.

Roasting & Peeling (Bell) Peppers

1 Leave the peppers whole or cut them in half and scrape out the cores and seeds. Place them on a grill (broiler) rack under medium heat, turning them occasionally, until the skins are evenly blistered and charred, but not too burnt, as this will make the flesh taste bitter.

2 Seal the peppers in a plastic bag or place them in a bowl and cover them with several sheets of kitchen paper. When the steam has softened them, peel off the skins. Remove the bitter seeds if necessary, working over a bowl to catch any juices. The juices can be used in a salad dressing.

Basic Recipes

The recipes in this book are largely complete in themselves, but there are a few basics that crop up again and again, such as tomato sauce and doughs for pizzas and pastas. You can, of course, substitute bought ingredients, such as sauces, ready-made pasta and pizza bases, but do make your own if you have time, as they taste great.

Pizza Dough
Makes I x 25–30cm/10–12in round pizza base

175g/6oz/1½ cups strong white bread flour
1.5ml/¼ tsp salt
5ml/1 tsp easy-blend (rapid-rise) dried yeast
120–150ml/4–5fl oz/½–⅔ cup
   lukewarm water

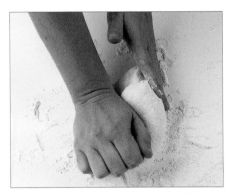

I Sift the flour and salt into a bowl and stir in the yeast. Add the water and mix to a soft dough. Knead on a lightly floured surface for 10 minutes, until smooth and elastic. Return to the clean bowl, cover with lightly oiled clear film (plastic wrap) and leave in a warm place for 1 hour, or until doubled in size.

2 Knock back (punch down) the dough, knead it for 2 minutes, then roll it out to a 25–30cm/10–12in round. Place on a greased baking sheet and knock up the edges. Top and bake as in the recipes.

> ### Cook's Tip
> Mix and knead the dough in a food processor, if you like, but transfer it to a bowl for rising.

Pasta Dough
Serves 6

300g/11oz/2¾ cups strong white bread flour
5ml/1 tsp salt
3 eggs, beaten

I Put the flour and salt in a food processor. Pour in one egg, cover and pulse to mix on maximum speed. Add the remaining eggs through the feeder tube and mix briefly to form a dough.

2 Knead the dough on a clean surface for 5 minutes if you are shaping it in a pasta machine; 10 minutes if shaping by hand. The dough should be very smooth and elastic. Wrap it in clear film (plastic wrap) and let it rest for 15–20 minutes before rolling and cutting it into shapes.

Making Pasta Dough by Hand

I Mound the flour on a work surface, make a well in the centre and add the eggs and salt. Mix with your hands or a fork, gradually incorporating the surrounding flour until a dough forms. Knead as in the main recipe.

French Dressing
Makes about 120ml/4fl oz/½ cup

90ml/6 tbsp mixed olive and sunflower oils
15ml/1 tbsp white wine vinegar
5ml/1 tsp French mustard
pinch of granulated sugar
salt and ground black pepper

Place the oil and vinegar in a screw-top jar. Add the mustard and sugar. Close the lid tightly and shake well. Season to taste.

Mayonnaise
Makes about 350ml/12fl oz/1½ cups

2 egg yolks
15ml/1 tbsp Dijon mustard
30ml/2 tbsp lemon juice or white wine vinegar
300ml/½ pint/1¼ cups sunflower oil
salt and ground black pepper

I Put the egg yolks, mustard, half the lemon juice or vinegar and a pinch of salt in a blender or food processor and process for 10 seconds to mix.

2 With the motor running, add the oil through the feeder tube, drop by drop at first and then in a steady stream until the mayonnaise is thick and creamy. Taste and sharpen with the remaining juice or vinegar and season to taste.

Tomato Sauce
Makes about 350ml/12fl oz/1½ cups

15ml/1 tbsp olive oil
1 onion, finely chopped
1 garlic clove, crushed
400g/14oz can chopped tomatoes
15ml/1 tbsp tomato purée (paste)
15ml/1 tbsp chopped fresh mixed herbs
pinch of sugar
salt and ground black pepper

I Heat the oil in a pan and cook the onion and garlic gently until softened. Stir in the tomatoes, tomato purée, herbs and sugar, with salt and pepper to taste.

2 Simmer, uncovered, for 15–20 minutes, stirring occasionally, until the mixture has reduced and is thick. Use immediately or cool, cover and store in the refrigerator.

ELEGANT SOUPS & APPETIZERS

The first course determines our expectations of a meal, so it is important that it looks tempting and delicious, as well as tasting wonderful. An appetizing aroma is an added bonus that is easily achieved with any of these lovely hot soups, such as Garlic & Coriander Soup, or tasty warm pastries, such as Cheese & Pesto Pasties. The aim is to stimulate the appetite, wake up the taste buds and encourage guests to anticipate the delights yet to come. So, if you are planning to serve a fairly light main course, choose a more substantial soup or appetizer to start, but avoid any recipes with a very robust or spicy flavour, which might overpower a delicate main dish. Recipes such as Borscht, Roasted Vegetable Soup and Brandied Roquefort Tarts would also be excellent on a cold winter's evening. By contrast, nothing makes a more refreshing and appetizing introduction to a summery, *al fresco* lunch than a creamy, chilled soup.

Of course, one of the main advantages to serving chilled soup or a cold appetizer is that it can be prepared in advance, freeing the cook to spend time with their guests. It also provides an appealing contrast if it is followed by a hot main course. You can achieve an exciting contrast in textures too – serve melt-in-the-mouth pastries or crisp, deep-fried fritters before crêpes or casseroles, and richly flavoured soups or elegant terrines before baked dishes, pies or tarts, for example.

Although there is no doubt that the soups and appetizers featured in this chapter are elegant and impressive, the recipes are actually very easy to follow and not especially time consuming – the perfect combination for a successful dinner party. Even those dishes that are served hot will not take you away from your guests for long. Some, such as Vermicelli with Lemon, take only 10 minutes to prepare and cook, while others, such as Wild Mushroom Soup, can be left to simmer gently while you share a pre-dinner drink.

Chilled Leek & Potato Soup

This creamy-smooth soup is served with a tangy yogurt topping that complements its subtle flavour.

Serves 4
25g/1oz/2 tbsp butter
15ml/1 tbsp vegetable oil
1 small onion, chopped
3 leeks, sliced
2 medium floury potatoes, diced
about 600ml/1 pint/2½ cups
   vegetable stock
about 300ml/ ½ pint/
   1¼ cups milk
45ml/3 tbsp single (light) cream
salt and ground black pepper
60ml/4 tbsp natural (plain) yogurt
   and fried chopped leeks,
   to serve

1 Heat the butter and oil in a large, heavy pan and add the onion, leeks and potatoes. Cover and cook over a low heat, stirring occasionally, for 15 minutes, until the vegetables have softened and the onion is golden.

2 Stir in the stock and milk. Bring to the boil, lower the heat, cover and simmer for 10 minutes.

3 Leave to cool slightly, then process the mixture, in batches if necessary, in a blender or a food processor to a purée. Pour the soup into a bowl, stir in the cream and season generously with salt and pepper.

4 Set the soup aside to cool, then cover and chill in the refrigerator for 3–4 hours. You may need to add a little extra milk or cold vegetable stock to thin the soup before serving, as it will thicken slightly as it cools.

5 Ladle the soup into chilled soup bowls and top each portion with a spoonful of yogurt and a sprinkling of fried leeks.

> **Cook's Tip**
> *You will need one or two thin young leeks for the garnish. Clean them, then slice them into rounds. Fry them in a mixture of butter and olive oil until they are crisp-tender.*

Chilled Coconut Soup

Refreshing, cooling and not too filling, this soup makes an excellent summer appetizer, but it could also be served after a spicy curry, to refresh the palate.

Serves 6
1.2 litres/2 pints/5 cups milk
225g/8oz/2⅔ cups unsweetened
   desiccated (dry unsweetened
   shredded) coconut
400ml/14fl oz/1⅔ cups coconut
   milk from a can or carton
400ml/14fl oz/1⅔ cups
   vegetable stock
200ml/7fl oz/scant 1 cup
   double (heavy) cream
2.5ml/ ½ tsp salt
2.5ml/ ½ tsp ground
   white pepper
5ml/1 tsp caster (superfine) sugar
small bunch of fresh
   coriander (cilantro)

1 Bring the milk to the boil in a large pan. Stir in the coconut, lower the heat and simmer, stirring occasionally, for 30 minutes. Spoon the mixture into a food processor and process until smooth. This may up to 5 minutes, so pause frequently and scrape down the sides of the bowl.

2 Rinse the pan, pour in the processed mixture and add the coconut milk. Stir in the stock, cream, salt, pepper and sugar. Bring to the boil, stirring occasionally, then lower the heat and cook for 10 minutes.

3 Reserve a few coriander leaves for the garnish, then chop the rest finely and stir them into the soup. Pour the soup into a large bowl, let it cool, then cover and chill in the refrigerator.

4 Just before serving, taste and adjust the seasoning. Serve in chilled bowls, garnished with the reserved coriander leaves.

> **Cook's Tips**
> • *Avoid using sweetened coconut, which would spoil the flavour of this soup.*
> • *Use a tasty vegetable stock, boiling it down if necessary to concentrate the flavour.*

Tomato & Fresh Basil Soup

This is the perfect choice for late summer, when fresh tomatoes are at their most flavoursome and sweet.

Serves 4–6
15ml/1 tbsp olive oil
25g/1oz/2 tbsp butter
1 medium onion, finely chopped
900g/2lb ripe Italian plum
  tomatoes, coarsely chopped
1 garlic clove, coarsely chopped
about 750ml/1¼ pints/3 cups
  vegetable stock
120ml/4fl oz/ ½ cup dry
  white wine
30ml/2 tbsp sun-dried
  tomato paste
30ml/2 tbsp shredded fresh basil,
  plus a few whole leaves,
  to garnish
150ml/ ¼ pint/ ⅔ cup
  double (heavy) cream
salt and ground black pepper

1 Heat the oil and butter in a large, heavy pan. Add the onion and cook over a low heat, stirring occasionally, for about 5 minutes, until softened and translucent but not browned.

2 Stir in the chopped tomatoes and garlic, then add the vegetable stock, white wine and sun-dried tomato paste and season with salt and pepper to taste. Bring to the boil, then lower the heat, half-cover the pan and simmer gently for 20 minutes, stirring occasionally.

3 Process the soup with the shredded basil in a blender or food processor, then press through a sieve into a clean pan.

4 Stir in the cream and heat through, stirring constantly. Do not allow the soup to boil. Check the consistency and flavour. Add more stock and seasoning if necessary. Ladle the soup into heated individual bowls and garnish with whole basil leaves. Serve immediately.

Variation
The soup can also be served chilled. Pour it into a container after sieving, cool, then chill in the refrigerator for at least 4 hours. Serve in chilled bowls.

Garlic & Coriander Soup

This simple soup should be made with the best ingredients – plump garlic, fresh coriander, high-quality crusty country bread and extra virgin olive oil.

Serves 6
25g/1oz/1 cup fresh coriander
  (cilantro), leaves and stalks
  chopped separately
1.5 litres/2½ pints/6¼ cups
  vegetable stock
5–6 plump garlic cloves, peeled
6 eggs
3 slices day-old white bread,
  crusts removed and torn into
  bitesize pieces
90ml/6 tbsp extra virgin olive oil,
  plus extra to serve
salt and ground black pepper

1 Place the coriander stalks in a pan. Add the stock and bring to the boil over a medium heat. Lower the heat and simmer gently for 10 minutes. Cool slightly, then process the mixture in a blender or food processor. Press through a sieve into the clean pan. Heat gently.

2 Crush the garlic with 5ml/1 tsp salt, then stir in 120ml/ 4fl oz/ ½ cup of the hot coriander stock. Return the mixture to the pan.

3 Bring the soup to the boil and season to taste with salt and pepper. Leave over a low heat. Poach the eggs.

4 Divide the pieces of bread among six soup plates or bowls and drizzle the olive oil over it. Stir the chopped coriander leaves into the soup, then ladle it over the bread. Stir each portion once, then add a poached egg to each bowl. Serve immediately, offering more olive oil at the table so that it can be drizzled over the soup to taste.

Cook's Tip
The olive oil is traditionally used to moisten the bread and flavour the soup, but you can use less than the recommended quantity if you like.

Pear & Watercress Soup

Pears and Stilton are classic companions, although they are seldom served in soup. Try this sophisticated appetizer – it is delicious.

Serves 6
1 bunch of watercress
4 medium pears, peeled and sliced
900ml/1½ pints/3¾ cups vegetable stock

120ml/4fl oz/½ cup double (heavy) cream
juice of 1 lime
salt and ground black pepper

For the Stilton croûtons
25g/1oz/2 tbsp butter
15ml/1 tbsp olive oil
3 slices day-old white bread, crusts removed, cubed
115g/4oz Stilton cheese

1 Reserve about one-third of the watercress leaves. Place the rest of the watercress leaves and the stalks in a large pan and add the pears and stock. Bring to the boil, then lower the heat and simmer for 15–20 minutes.

2 Leave the mixture to cool slightly, then pour it into a food processor. Add most of the reserved watercress leaves, reserving some for garnishing, and blend until smooth. Scrape the mixture into the clean pan and stir in the cream and lime juice. Season to taste with salt and pepper.

3 Make the croûtons. Melt the butter and oil and fry the bread cubes until golden brown. Drain on kitchen paper, then spread out in a shallow flameproof dish. Crumble the Stilton on top and heat under a hot grill (broiler) until bubbling.

4 Meanwhile, reheat the soup gently, stirring constantly. Pour it into heated bowls. Divide the croûtons and remaining watercress among the bowls and serve immediately.

Cook's Tip
Watercress does not keep well, so use it within a day of purchase. Otherwise, the leaves will wilt and turn yellow.

Asparagus Soup

Home-made asparagus soup has a delicate flavour, quite unlike that from a can.

Serves 4
450g/1lb young asparagus
40g/1½oz/3 tbsp butter
6 shallots, sliced
15g/½oz/2 tbsp plain (all-purpose) flour

600ml/1 pint/2½ cups vegetable stock
15ml/1 tbsp lemon juice
250ml/8fl oz/1 cup milk
120ml/4fl oz/½ cup single (light) cream
salt and ground black pepper
10ml/2 tsp chopped fresh chervil, to garnish

1 Trim the stalks of the asparagus if necessary. Cut 4cm/1½in off the tops of half the asparagus and set aside for a garnish. Slice the remaining asparagus.

2 Melt 25g/1oz/2 tbsp of the butter in a large, heavy pan. Add the shallots and cook over a low heat, stirring occasionally, for 2–3 minutes, until softened and translucent but not brown.

3 Add the sliced asparagus and cook over a gentle heat for about 1 minute. Stir in the flour and cook, stirring constantly, for 1 minute. Stir in the stock and lemon juice and season to taste with salt and pepper. Bring to the boil, then lower the heat and simmer, partially covered, for 15–20 minutes, until the asparagus is very tender.

4 Cool the soup slightly, then process the mixture with the milk in a blender or food processor until smooth. Press the purée through a sieve into a clean pan.

5 Melt the remaining butter in a frying pan over a low heat. Add the reserved asparagus tips and cook gently for about 3–4 minutes, until softened.

6 Reheat the soup gently for 3–4 minutes, until piping hot. Stir in the cream and the asparagus tips. Ladle the soup into heated individual bowls, sprinkle with the chopped fresh chervil and serve immediately.

Borscht

Beetroot is the main ingredient of this classic Russian soup, which is also very popular throughout Eastern Europe.

Serves 4–6

40g/1½oz/3 tbsp butter
2 onions, sliced
900g/2lb raw beetroot (beet), peeled and cut into thick batons
2 carrots, cut into thick batons
2 celery sticks, cut into thick batons
2 garlic cloves, crushed
4 tomatoes, peeled, seeded and chopped
bouquet garni
4 whole peppercorns
1.2 litres/2 pints/5 cups vegetable stock
150ml/¼ pint/⅔ cup beetroot (beet) kvas (see Cook's Tip) or the liquid from a jar of pickled beetroot (beet)
salt and ground black pepper
sour cream and chopped fresh chives, to garnish

1 Melt the butter in a large, heavy pan and cook the onions over a low heat for 5 minutes, stirring occasionally. Add the beetroot, carrots and celery and cook for 5 minutes more, stirring occasionally.

2 Stir in the garlic and chopped tomatoes and continue to cook, stirring frequently, for 2 minutes more.

3 Add the bouquet garni, peppercorns and stock. Bring to the boil, lower the heat, cover and simmer for 1¼ hours, until all the vegetables are tender. Discard the bouquet garni. Stir in the beetroot kvas and season to taste. Bring to the boil. Ladle into bowls and serve with sour cream sprinkled with chives.

Cook's Tip
Beetroot (beet) kvas, fermented beetroot juice, adds an intense colour and a slight tartness. If unavailable, peel and grate 1 beetroot, add 150ml/¼ pint/⅔ cup vegetable stock and 10ml/2 tsp lemon juice. Bring to the boil, cover and remove from the heat. Leave for 30 minutes. Strain before using.

Wild Mushroom Soup

Dried porcini mushrooms have an intense flavour, so a small quantity is sufficient to give this soup a truly superb taste.

Serves 4

25g/1oz/1 cup dried porcini mushrooms
250ml/8fl oz/1 cup warm water
30ml/2 tbsp olive oil
15g/½oz/1 tbsp butter
2 leeks, thinly sliced
2 shallots, coarsely chopped
1 garlic clove, coarsely chopped
225g/8oz/3 cups fresh wild mushrooms
about 1.2 litres/2 pints/5 cups vegetable stock
2.5ml/½ tsp dried thyme
150ml/¼ pint/⅔ cup double (heavy) cream
salt and ground black pepper
fresh thyme sprigs, to garnish

1 Soak the dried porcini in the warm water for 20–30 minutes. Lift out of the liquid and squeeze out as much of the liquid as possible. Strain all the liquid and reserve. Chop the mushrooms.

2 Heat the oil and butter in a large pan and cook the leeks, shallots and garlic gently for about 5 minutes, stirring frequently.

3 Slice the fresh mushrooms and add them to the pan. Stir over a medium heat until they begin to soften, then pour in the stock and bring to the boil. Add the porcini, soaking liquid and dried thyme and season to taste. Lower the heat, half-cover the pan and simmer gently for 30 minutes, stirring occasionally.

4 Process three-quarters of the soup in a blender or food processor until smooth. Return it to the pan, stir in the cream and heat through. Add more stock if the soup is too thick. Taste for seasoning. Serve hot, garnished with the thyme sprigs.

Cook's Tip
Look for packets of fresh mixed wild mushrooms in the supermarket. Use them on the day of purchase, if possible, as they don't keep well.

Roasted Vegetable Soup

Roasting the vegetables gives this winter soup a wonderful depth of flavour.

Serves 6
60ml/4 tbsp olive oil
1 small butternut squash, peeled, seeded and cubed
2 carrots, cut into thick rounds
1 large parsnip, cubed
1 small swede (rutabaga), cubed
2 leeks, thickly sliced
1 onion, quartered
3 bay leaves
4 fresh thyme sprigs, plus extra to garnish
3 fresh rosemary sprigs
1.2 litres/2 pints/5 cups vegetable stock
salt and ground black pepper
sour cream, to serve

1 Preheat the oven to 200°C/400°F/Gas 6. Put the olive oil into a large bowl. Add the vegetables and toss until well coated.

2 Spread out the vegetables in a single layer on one large or two small baking sheets. Tuck the bay leaves and thyme and rosemary sprigs among the vegetables.

3 Roast the vegetables for about 50 minutes, until tender, turning them occasionally to make sure that they brown evenly. Remove from the oven, discard the herbs and transfer the vegetables to a large pan.

4 Pour the stock into the pan and bring to the boil. Lower the heat, season to taste with salt and pepper, then simmer for 10 minutes. Transfer the soup to a food processor or blender and process for a few minutes until thick and smooth.

5 Return the soup to the pan and heat through. Season well. Serve in heated bowls, adding a swirl of sour cream to each portion. Garnish with the extra thyme sprigs.

Cook's Tip
A hand-held blender makes short work of puréeing the soup and saves time on the clearing up.

Spicy Peanut Soup

When you serve a lot of soups, it is good to have some more unusual recipes in your repertoire. This one comes from Africa and it tastes delicious.

Serves 6
30ml/2 tbsp vegetable oil
1 large onion, finely chopped
2 garlic cloves, crushed
5ml/1 tsp mild chilli powder
225g/8oz carrots, finely chopped
2 red (bell) peppers, seeded and finely chopped
225g/8oz potatoes, finely chopped
3 celery sticks, sliced
900ml/1½ pints/3¾ cups vegetable stock
90ml/6 tbsp crunchy peanut butter
115g/4oz/⅔ cup corn kernels
salt and ground black pepper
coarsely chopped unsalted roasted peanuts, to garnish

1 Heat the oil in a large, heavy pan. Add the onion and garlic and cook, stirring occasionally, for about 3 minutes, until softened and translucent. Stir in the chilli powder and cook for 1 minute more.

2 Add the carrots, peppers, potatoes and celery. Stir well, then cook for 4 minutes more, stirring occasionally.

3 Add the stock, peanut butter and corn and stir well until thoroughly combined.

4 Season to taste with salt and pepper. Bring to the boil, lower the heat, cover and simmer for about 20 minutes, or until the vegetables are tender.

5 Adjust the seasoning, if necessary. Ladle the soup into heated bowls, sprinkle with the chopped peanuts and serve.

Cook's Tip
Different brands of chilli powder vary in strength, so it is best to use it with caution to begin with. Some varieties also include added ingredients, which may not go with your recipe.

Grilled Goat's Cheese Salad

The fresh tangy flavour of goat's cheese contrasts beautifully with the mild salad leaves in this satisfying and attractive appetizer.

Serves 4
2 firm round whole goat's cheeses, about 65–115g/ 2½–4oz each
4 slices French bread
extra virgin olive oil, for drizzling

175g/6oz ready-to-serve mixed salad leaves
chopped fresh chives, to garnish

For the vinaigrette dressing
½ garlic clove
5ml/1 tsp Dijon mustard
5ml/1 tsp white wine vinegar
5ml/1 tsp dry white wine
45ml/3 tbsp extra virgin olive oil
salt and ground black pepper

1 To make the dressing, rub a large salad bowl with the cut side of the garlic clove. Combine the mustard, vinegar and wine in the bowl. Add salt and pepper to taste, then whisk in the oil, 15ml/1 tbsp at a time, to form a thick vinaigrette.

2 Using a sharp knife, cut the goat's cheeses in half across their width to make four "cakes".

3 Arrange the bread slices in a grill (broiler) pan and toast them on one side under a hot grill. Turn them over and place a piece of cheese, cut side up, on each slice. Drizzle with olive oil and grill (broil) until the cheese is lightly browned.

4 Add the leaves to the salad bowl and toss to coat with the dressing. Divide the salad among four plates, top each with a goat's cheese croûton and garnish with chives, then serve.

Cook's Tip
The best-known goat's cheeses are French, known generically as chèvre and also sold under specific names, such as Crottin de Chavignol. There are other excellent goat's milk cheeses, such as the English Cerney, Capricorn Goat and Vulscombe, and Caprile Banon and Chèvre de Provence from the United States.

Asparagus in Egg & Lemon Sauce

As an appetizer or even a light lunch, fresh asparagus is a special treat, particularly when topped with a tangy, fresh-tasting sauce.

Serves 4
675g/1½lb asparagus
15ml/1 tbsp cornflour (cornstarch)
10ml/2 tsp granulated sugar
2 egg yolks
juice of 1½ lemons
salt

1 Trim the asparagus stalks, discarding the tough ends, then tie them in a bundle. Cook in a tall pan of lightly salted, boiling water over a medium heat for 7–10 minutes.

2 Drain well, reserving 200ml/7fl oz/scant 1 cup of the cooking liquid. Untie the asparagus stalks and arrange them in a shallow serving dish.

3 Put the cornflour in a small pan. Stir in enough of the reserved cooking liquid to form a smooth paste, then stir in the remainder. Bring to the boil, stirring constantly, and cook over a low heat until the sauce thickens slightly. Stir in the sugar, remove the pan from the heat and leave to cool slightly.

4 Beat the egg yolks with the lemon juice. Gradually stir the mixture into the cooled sauce. Cook over a very low heat, stirring constantly, until the sauce is fairly thick. Immediately remove the pan from the heat. Continue stirring for 1 minute.

5 Taste the sauce and add salt or sugar if needed. Let it cool slightly, then pour a little over the asparagus. Cover and chill for at least 2 hours before serving with the rest of the sauce.

Variation
This sauce goes very well with all sorts of young vegetables. Try it with baby leeks, cooked whole or chopped, or serve it with other baby vegetables, such as carrots.

Baby Onions & Mushrooms à la Grecque

There are many variations of this classic dish. The mushrooms may be omitted, but they add immeasurably to the flavour.

Serves 4
2 carrots
350g/12oz baby (pearl) onions
60ml/4 tbsp olive oil
120ml/4fl oz/ ½ cup dry
   white wine
5ml/1 tsp coriander seeds,
   lightly crushed
2 bay leaves
pinch of cayenne pepper
1 garlic clove, crushed
350g/12oz/4 cups
   button (white) mushrooms
3 tomatoes, peeled, seeded
   and quartered
salt and ground black pepper
45ml/3 tbsp chopped fresh
   parsley, to garnish
crusty bread, to serve

1 Peel the carrots and cut them into small dice. Peel the baby onions and trim the tops and roots.

2 Heat 45ml/3 tbsp of the olive oil in a deep frying pan. Add the carrots and onions and cook, stirring occasionally, for about 20 minutes, until the vegetables have browned lightly.

3 Add the white wine, coriander seeds, bay leaves, cayenne, garlic, button mushrooms and tomatoes, with salt and pepper to taste. Cook, uncovered, for 20–30 minutes, until the vegetables are soft and the sauce has thickened.

4 Transfer to a serving dish and leave to cool. Cover and chill until needed. Before serving, pour over the remaining olive oil and sprinkle with the parsley. Serve with crusty bread.

> **Cook's Tip**
> Don't trim too much from either the top or root end of the onions: if you do, the centres will pop out during cooking.

Marinated Vegetable Antipasto

If you ever want to prove just how delectable vegetables can be, serve this sensational selection of Italian-style appetizers.

Serves 4
For the (bell) peppers
3 red (bell) peppers, halved
   and seeded
3 yellow (bell) peppers, halved
   and seeded
4 garlic cloves, sliced
a handful of fresh basil leaves,
   plus extra to garnish
extra virgin olive oil
salt

For the mushrooms
450g/1lb/6 cups open
   cap mushrooms
60ml/4 tbsp extra virgin olive oil

1 large garlic clove, crushed
15ml/1 tbsp chopped
   fresh rosemary
250ml/8fl oz/1 cup dry
   white wine
salt and ground black pepper
fresh rosemary sprigs, to garnish

For the olives
120ml/4fl oz/ ½ cup extra virgin
   olive oil
1 dried red chilli
grated rind of 1 lemon
225g/8oz/1 ¼ cups Italian
   black olives
30ml/2 tbsp chopped fresh flat
   leaf parsley
1 lemon wedge, to serve

1 Place the pepper halves, skin side up, on a grill (broiler) rack and cook until the skins have charred. Transfer to a bowl and cover with crumpled kitchen paper. Leave to cool slightly.

2 When the pepper halves are cool enough to handle, peel off their skins, then cut the flesh into strips. Place the strips in a bowl and add the sliced garlic and basil leaves. Sprinkle over salt to taste, cover with olive oil and set aside to marinate for 3–4 hours, tossing occasionally. Chill in the refrigerator.

3 Slice the mushrooms thickly and place them in a large heatproof bowl. Heat the oil in a small pan and add the garlic and rosemary. Pour in the wine. Bring to the boil, then lower the heat and simmer for 3 minutes. Season to taste.

4 Pour the mixture over the mushrooms. Mix thoroughly and set aside until cool, stirring occasionally. Cover and leave to marinate overnight in the refrigerator.

5 Prepare the olives. Place the oil in a small pan and crumble in the chilli. Add the lemon rind. Heat gently for about 3 minutes. Add the olives and heat for 1 minute more. Tip into a bowl and leave to cool. Set aside to marinate overnight.

6 Let the marinated mushrooms come to room temperature before serving. Garnish them with rosemary sprigs. Garnish the chilled peppers with basil leaves. Sprinkle the olives with parsley and serve with the lemon wedge.

> **Cook's Tip**
> The (bell) pepper antipasto can be stored in a screw-top jar in the refrigerator for up to 2 weeks.

Stuffed Vine Leaves

Whether you serve these as part of a meze or as a solo appetizer, they are certain to prove popular.

Makes about 40
40 fresh vine (grape) leaves
60ml/4 tbsp olive oil
lemon wedges and a crisp salad,
   to serve

For the stuffing
150g/5oz/ ¾ cup long grain
   rice, rinsed
2 bunches of spring onions
   (scallions), finely chopped
40g/1½oz/⅓ cup pine nuts
45ml/3 tbsp seedless raisins
30ml/2 tbsp chopped fresh
   mint leaves
60ml/4 tbsp chopped
   fresh parsley
4ml/ ¾ tsp ground black pepper
salt

1 Using a knife or a pair of scissors, snip out the thick, coarse stems from the vine leaves. Blanch the leaves in a large pan of boiling salted water until they just begin to change colour. Drain, refresh in cold water, then drain again.

2 To make the stuffing, mix all the ingredients together in a bowl and season to taste with salt. Open out the vine leaves, ribbed side uppermost. Place a heaped teaspoonful of the stuffing on each.

3 Fold over the two outer edges to secure the stuffing, then roll up each vine leaf from the stem end to form a neat roll.

4 Arrange the stuffed vine leaves neatly in a steamer and sprinkle over the olive oil. Steam over boiling water for 50–60 minutes, or until the rice is completely cooked. Serve cold, but not chilled, with lemon wedges and a salad.

Cook's Tip
If you can't obtain fresh vine (grape) leaves, use two packets of vine leaves preserved in brine. Rinse and drain them well, then pat dry with kitchen paper before filling.

Vermicelli with Lemon

Fresh and tangy, this makes an excellent first course for a dinner party. It has the additional advantage of being extremely quick and easy to prepare.

Serves 4
350g/12oz dried vermicelli
juice of 2 large lemons

50g/2oz/ ¼ cup butter
200ml/7fl oz/scant 1 cup
   double (heavy) cream
15ml/1 tablespoon finely grated
   lemon rind
115g/4oz/1⅓ cups freshly grated
   Parmesan cheese
salt and ground black pepper

1 Cook the vermicelli in a large pan of lightly salted, boiling water until *al dente*.

2 Meanwhile, pour the lemon juice into a medium pan. Add the butter and cream, then stir in the lemon rind. Season with salt and pepper to taste.

3 Bring to the boil, stirring frequently. Lower the heat and simmer, stirring occasionally, for about 5 minutes, until the cream has reduced slightly.

4 Drain the pasta and return it to the pan. Add the grated Parmesan to the sauce, then taste for seasoning and adjust if necessary. Pour the sauce over the pasta. Toss quickly over a medium heat until the pasta is evenly coated with the sauce, then divide among four warmed bowls and serve immediately.

Cook's Tips
• *Lemons vary in the amount of juice they yield. On average, a large fresh lemon will yield 60–90ml/4–6 tbsp. The lemony flavour of this dish is quite pronounced – you can use less juice if you like.*
• *Try to find unwaxed lemons if you are going to grate the rind. (Waxed lemons have been treated with diphenyl to preserve the rind.) Otherwise, wash the lemons thoroughly first.*

Vegetable Terrine with Brandy

A feast for the eye and the palate – that's this luscious layer of brandy-flavoured custard and a colourful combination of vegetables.

Serves 4
vegetable oil, for greasing
1 red (bell) pepper, quartered
    and seeded
1 green (bell) pepper, quartered
    and seeded
75g/3oz/ ¾ cup fresh or
    frozen peas
6 fresh green asparagus stalks
2 carrots, cut into batons
150ml/ ¼ pint/ ⅔ cup milk
150ml/ ¼ pint/ ⅔ cup double
    (heavy) cream
6 eggs, beaten
15ml/1 tbsp brandy
175g/6oz/ ¾ cup low-fat
    soft cheese
15ml/1 tbsp chopped
    fresh parsley
salt and ground black pepper
salad leaves, cucumber slices and
    halved tomatoes, to serve

1 Preheat the oven to 180°C/350°F/Gas 4. Grease and base-line a 900g/2lb loaf tin (pan). Place the peppers, skin side up, on a grill (broiler) rack and cook until the skins have charred. Transfer to a bowl and cover with crumpled kitchen paper.

2 Cook the peas, asparagus and carrots in separate pans of lightly salted, boiling water until tender. Drain and dry on kitchen paper. Peel off the skins from the pepper quarters.

3 In a bowl, combine the milk, cream, eggs, brandy, soft cheese and parsley. Mix well and season with plenty of salt and pepper.

4 Arrange some of the vegetables in the base of the loaf tin, trimming to fit if necessary. Spoon some of the cheese mixture over the vegetables. Continue layering the vegetables and the cheese mixture, ending with a layer of peppers. Cover the tin with foil and stand it in a roasting pan. Pour in boiling water to come halfway up the sides of the loaf tin.

5 Bake for 45 minutes, or until the custard is just firm. Leave the terrine in the tin until cold, then remove it from the roasting tin. Invert it on to a plate. Lift off the lining paper and slice the terrine. Serve with the salad leaves, cucumber and tomatoes.

Aubergine & Spinach Terrines

These individual terrines make an elegant first course.

Serves 4
1 aubergine (eggplant)
30ml/2 tbsp extra virgin olive oil
2 courgettes (zucchini),
    thinly sliced
leaves from 1 fresh thyme sprig
4 tomatoes, peeled and seeded
4 fresh basil leaves, thinly sliced
275g/10oz fresh baby
    spinach leaves
1 garlic clove, crushed
15g/ ½oz/1 tbsp butter
pinch of freshly grated nutmeg
salt and ground black pepper
½ roasted red (bell) pepper,
    skinned and chopped, plus a
    little balsamic vinegar, to serve

1 Preheat the oven to 190°C/375°F/Gas 5. Cover one end of four 6cm/2½in diameter metal muffin rings with clear film (plastic wrap) to seal.

2 Slice the aubergine into four equal rounds. Heat half the oil in a frying pan and cook the aubergine slices on both sides until brown. Place them on a baking sheet and cook in the oven for 10 minutes. Transfer to a plate lined with kitchen paper.

3 Heat half the remaining oil in the same pan and cook the courgettes for 2 minutes, then drain on the kitchen paper. Season with salt and pepper and sprinkle with thyme leaves.

4 Place the tomatoes, basil and remaining oil in a heavy frying pan and cook for 5–8 minutes. Cook the spinach, garlic and butter in a pan, allowing all the water to evaporate. Drain well, add the nutmeg, then season with salt and pepper.

5 Line the base and 1cm/ ½in of the sides of the muffin rings with the spinach leaves, leaving no gaps. Place courgette slices around the edges of each ring, overlapping them slightly. Divide the tomato mixture equally among the rings, pressing it down well. Place the aubergines on the top, trimming the edges to fit.

6 Seal the top with clear film and pierce the base to allow any liquid to escape. Chill overnight. Remove from the rings and serve with roasted pepper, drizzled with balsamic vinegar.

Vegetable Tempura

These deep-fried fritters are based on *Kaki-age*, a popular Japanese dish.

Makes 8
2 medium courgettes (zucchini)
$^1/_2$ medium aubergine (eggplant)
1 large carrot
$^1/_2$ small Spanish (Bermuda) onion
vegetable oil, for deep-frying

salt and ground black pepper
sea salt flakes, lemon slices and
    Japanese soy sauce, to serve

For the batter
1 egg
120ml/4fl oz/ $^1/_2$ cup iced water
115g/4oz/1 cup plain (all-
    purpose) flour

1 Using a vegetable peeler, pare strips of peel from the courgettes and aubergine to give a stripy effect. Cut the courgettes, aubergine and carrot into strips about 7.5–10cm/3–4in long and 3mm/$^1/_8$in wide and put them in a colander.

2 Sprinkle the vegetable strips liberally with salt. Leave for about 30 minutes, then rinse thoroughly under cold running water. Drain well.

3 Thinly slice the onion from top to base, discarding the plump pieces in the middle. Separate the layers so that there are lots of fine long strips. Mix all the vegetables together and season to taste with salt and pepper.

4 Make the batter immediately before frying: mix the egg and iced water in a bowl, then sift in the flour. Mix very briefly with a fork or chopsticks – the batter should remain lumpy. Add the vegetables to the batter and mix to combine.

5 Half-fill a wok with oil and heat to 180°C/350°F or until a cube of day-old bread browns in 60 seconds. Scoop up a heaped tablespoon of the mixture at a time and carefully lower it into the oil to make a fritter. Deep-fry, in batches, for about 3 minutes, until golden brown and crisp.

6 Drain the fritters on kitchen paper and serve, offering each diner sea salt flakes, lemon slices and soy sauce for dipping.

Spring Onion & Ricotta Fritters

These melt-in-the-mouth fritters make an unusual appetizer and are very tasty, especially if you serve them with a spicy avocado salsa.

Serves 4–6
250g/9oz/generous 1 cup
    ricotta cheese
1 large (US extra large)
    egg, beaten
90ml/6 tbsp self-raising (self-
    rising) flour
90ml/6 tbsp milk
1 bunch of spring onions
    (scallions), thinly sliced

30ml/2 tbsp chopped fresh
    coriander (cilantro)
sunflower oil, for frying
salt and ground black pepper

To garnish
fresh coriander (cilantro) sprigs
lime wedges

To serve
Avocado & Tomato
    Dipping Sauce
200ml/7fl oz/scant 1 cup
    crème fraîche

1 Beat the ricotta in a bowl until smooth, then beat in the egg and flour, followed by the milk to make a smooth, thick batter. Beat in the spring onions and coriander. Season to taste.

2 Heat a little oil in a non-stick frying pan over a medium heat. Add spoonfuls of the mixture, in batches, to make fritters about 7.5cm/3in across. Fry for 4–5 minutes each side, until set and browned. The mixture makes 12 fritters.

3 Drain the fritters on kitchen paper and serve immediately. Garnish with the coriander sprigs and lime wedges, and serve with the dipping sauce and crème fraîche.

> **Cook's Tip**
> It is important that the ricotta is well beaten before the other ingredients are added to make the batter. Once the flour has been added, beat lightly, just to make sure that it is thoroughly combined. Over-beating will make the fritters stodgy.

Avocado & Tomato Dipping Sauce

This tastes superb with the Spring Onion & Ricotta Fritters, but can also be served with fried potato skins, crudités, pretzels or breadsticks.

Serves 4–6
2 ripe, but not soft, avocados
1 small red onion, diced

grated rind and juice of 1 lime
$^1/_2$–1 fresh green or red chilli,
    seeded and finely chopped
225g/8oz tomatoes, peeled,
    seeded and diced
30–45ml/2–3 tbsp chopped
    mixed fresh mint and
    coriander (cilantro)
pinch of caster (superfine) sugar
salt and ground black pepper

1 Peel, stone (pit) and dice the avocados. Place in a bowl with the red onion, lime rind and juice. Add chilli to taste, the tomatoes, mint and coriander. Season, then stir in the sugar.
2 Cover closely and set aside for 30 minutes before using.

Twice Baked Gruyère & Potato Soufflés

These were all the rage a few years ago and should not be forgotten. Easily prepared in advance, they are perfect for entertaining.

Serves 4
butter, for greasing
225g/8oz floury potatoes

2 eggs, separated
175g/6oz/1½ cups grated
　Gruyère cheese
50g/2oz/½ cup self-raising (self-
　rising) flour
50g/2oz fresh young spinach
　leaves, finely chopped
salt and ground black pepper
salad leaves, to serve

1 Preheat the oven to 200°C/400°F/Gas 6. Grease four large ramekins. Cook the potatoes in lightly salted, boiling water for 20 minutes, until very tender. Drain thoroughly and mash with the egg yolks.

2 Stir in half the Gruyère cheese and all the flour. Season to taste with salt and pepper, then fold in the spinach.

3 Whisk the egg whites until they form soft peaks. Stir a little of the egg white into the spinach mixture to loosen it slightly, then fold in the remainder.

4 Place the ramekins on a baking sheet. Divide the mixture among them. Bake for 20 minutes. Remove from the oven and leave to cool.

5 Reheat the oven to 200°C/400°F/Gas 6. Carefully invert the soufflés on to a baking sheet and sprinkle with the remaining Gruyère cheese. Bake for 5 minutes. Serve immediately with salad leaves.

> **Variation**
> *For a different flavouring, try replacing the Gruyère with a crumbled blue cheese, such as Stilton.*

Cheese & Pesto Pasties

Dispense with a formal appetizer and serve these with drinks instead. They are also perfect for parties.

Serves 8
225g/8oz frozen
　chopped spinach
30ml/2 tbsp pine nuts

60ml/4 tbsp pesto sauce
115g/4oz/1 cup grated
　Gruyère cheese
50g/2oz/⅔ cup freshly grated
　Parmesan cheese
2 x 275g/10oz packets frozen filo
　pastry, thawed
30ml/2 tbsp olive oil
salt and ground black pepper

1 Preheat the oven to 190°C/375°F/Gas 5. Prepare the filling. Put the frozen spinach into a pan. Heat it gently, breaking it up as it thaws. Increase the heat to drive off any excess moisture. Transfer to a bowl and cool.

2 Spread out the pine nuts in a frying pan and stir over a very low heat until they are lightly toasted. Chop them and add them to the spinach, with the pesto. Stir in the Gruyère and Parmesan cheeses. Season to taste with salt and pepper.

3 Keeping the rest of the filo pastry covered, cut one sheet into 5cm/2in wide strips. Brush each strip with oil. Put a teaspoon of filling on one end of a strip of pastry. Fold the end over in a triangle, enclosing the filling.

4 Continue to fold the triangle over and over again until the end of the strip is reached. Repeat with the other strips, until all the filling has been used up.

5 Place the pasties on baking sheets, brush them with oil and bake for 20–25 minutes, or until golden brown. Cool slightly on a wire rack. Serve warm.

> **Cook's Tip**
> *Keep the filo moist and pliable by keeping it covered with clear film (plastic wrap) or a damp dishtowel.*

Quail's Egg & Vermouth Tartlets

The hard-boiled eggs have an attractive marbled surface.

Serves 4
10 quail's eggs
30ml/2 tbsp soy sauce
30ml/2 tbsp mustard seeds
15ml/1 tbsp green tea leaves
6 filo pastry sheets, thawed
   if frozen

50g/2oz/ ¼ cup butter, melted
1 small avocado
45ml/3 tbsp dry white vermouth
30ml/2 tbsp Mayonnaise
10ml/2 tsp freshly squeezed
   lime juice
salt and ground black pepper
paprika, for dusting
lamb's lettuce (corn salad),
   to serve

1 Put the quail's eggs into a pan. Pour over cold water to cover. Add the soy sauce, mustard seeds and tea leaves. Bring to the boil, then lower the heat and simmer for 3 minutes.

2 Remove the pan from the heat and lift out the eggs with a slotted spoon. Gently tap them on a firm surface so that the shells crack all over. Put the eggs back into the liquid and leave in a cool place for 8 hours, or overnight.

3 Preheat the oven to 190°C/375°F/Gas 5. Grease four 10cm/4in tartlet cases. Brush each sheet of filo pastry with a little melted butter and stack the six sheets on top of each other. Stamp out four rounds with a 15cm/6in cutter.

4 Line the tartlet cases with the pastry and frill the edge of each. Put a crumpled piece of foil in each filo case (shell) and bake for 12–15 minutes, until cooked and golden. Remove the foil and set the cases aside to cool.

5 Cut the avocado in half, remove the stone (pit) and scoop the flesh into a blender or food processor. Add the vermouth, mayonnaise and lime juice and season to taste with salt and pepper. Process until smooth.

6 Shell and halve the eggs. Pipe or spoon the avocado mixture into the pastry cases and arrange the eggs on top. Dust them with a little paprika and serve, with the lamb's lettuce.

Brandied Roquefort Tarts

Light puff pastry rounds are topped with the irresistible combination of brandy and Roquefort cheese.

Makes 6
150g/5oz Roquefort cheese
30ml/2 tbsp brandy
30ml/2 tbsp olive oil
2 red onions (total weight about
   225g/8oz), thinly sliced

225g/8oz puff pastry, thawed
   if frozen
plain (all-purpose) flour,
   for dusting
beaten egg or milk, to glaze
6 walnut halves, chopped
30ml/2 tbsp chopped fresh chives
salt and ground black pepper
chive knots, to garnish
salad leaves, diced cucumber and
   thin tomato wedges, to serve

1 Crumble the Roquefort into a small bowl, pour the brandy over and leave to marinate for 1 hour. Meanwhile, heat the oil in a frying pan and cook the onions gently for 20 minutes, stirring occasionally. Set the pan aside.

2 Preheat the oven to 220°C/425°F/Gas 7. Grease a baking sheet. Roll out the pastry on a floured surface to a 5mm/¼in thickness and stamp out six rounds with a 10cm/4in fluted cutter. Put them on the baking sheet and prick with a fork.

3 Brush the edges of the pastry with a little beaten egg or milk. Add the walnuts and chives to the onion mixture and season with salt and pepper to taste. Divide the mixture among the pastry shapes, leaving the edges clear.

4 Spoon the brandied cheese mixture on top of the pastries and bake for 12–15 minutes, until golden. Serve warm, garnished with chive knots, on a bed of salad leaves, diced cucumber and thin tomato wedges.

Cook's Tip
To make the chive knots, simply tie chives together in groups of three, with a central knot. Blanch the chives briefly if they are not very pliable.

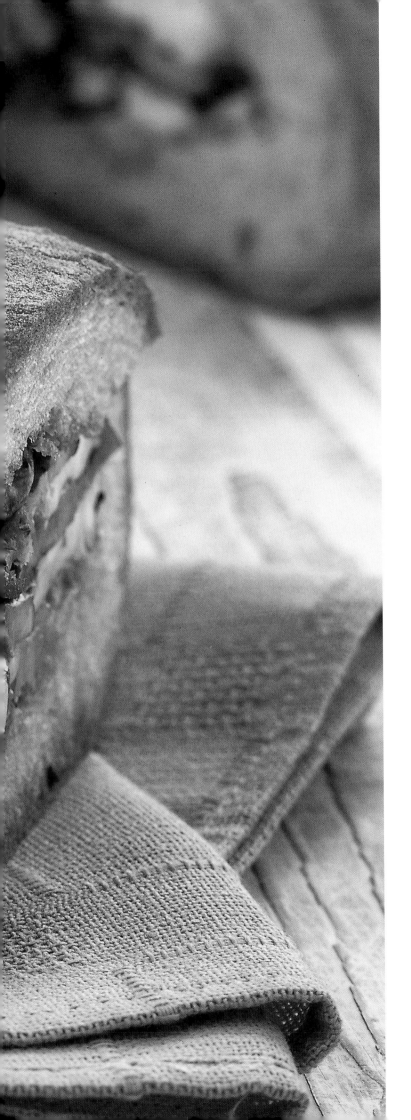

PARTY PIECES, PICNICS, BRUNCHES & LIGHT LUNCHES

Not all celebrations and special occasions call for a formal dinner party, but most are much more enjoyable with a selection of edible treats and tasty morsels. The fabulous recipes in this chapter can be adapted for all kinds of events, from a barbecue in the garden to a picnic at the coast, and from a Sunday brunch to a cocktail party. There are pâtés and terrines, egg dishes, cheese bites, fritters, fondues, roulades and soufflés, not to mention mouthwatering variations on the traditional sandwich that will add a professional touch to any buffet table. Depending on the occasion, how much time you have and the number of guests, you can mix and match hot and cold dishes, finger foods and more traditional platefuls.

Recipes range from classic dishes, such as that popular standby for a brunch party, Eggs Benedict with Quick Hollandaise, to innovative and exciting new ideas, such as Artichoke Rice Cakes with Melting Manchego. There are also some imaginative variations on tried and tested themes, such as Goat's Cheese & Gin Crostini and Nutty Mushroom Pâté. In fact, there is something for all tastes, occasions and times of year, from hot and spicy to crisp and crunchy and from subtle and sophisticated to robust and filling.

Many of these dishes can be prepared in advance and either served cold or assembled at the last minute to be popped in the oven or under the grill (broiler) when your guests arrive. The number of servings can be increased to cater for larger numbers simply by doubling or trebling the quantities. A good way to keep the party going when you are entertaining informally is to prepare food in batches – both hot and cold dishes – so as more guests arrive, fresh serving platters appear as if by magic. This will also allow you lots of opportunities to circulate and enjoy yourself without being stuck in the kitchen – so the occasion is special for you, too.

Nutty Mushroom Pâté

Spread this delicious, medium-textured pâté on chunks of crusty French bread and eat with crisp leaves of lettuce and sweet cherry tomatoes.

Serves 4–6

15ml/1 tbsp sunflower oil
1 onion, chopped
1 garlic clove, crushed
30ml/2 tbsp water
15ml/1 tbsp dry sherry
225g/8oz/3 cups button (white) mushrooms, chopped
75g/3oz/ ¾ cup cashew nuts or walnuts, chopped
150g/5oz/ ⅔ cup low-fat soft cheese
15ml/1 tbsp soy sauce
few dashes of vegetarian Worcestershire sauce
salt and ground black pepper
chopped fresh parsley and a little paprika, to garnish

1 Heat the oil in a pan. Add the onion and garlic and cook over a medium heat, stirring occasionally, for 3 minutes. Stir in the water, sherry and mushrooms. Cook, stirring constantly, for about 5 minutes. Season to taste with salt and pepper. Remove the pan from the heat and leave to cool a little.

2 Put the mixture into a food processor and add the cashew nuts or walnuts, cheese, soy sauce and Worcestershire sauce. Process to a coarse purée – do not allow the mixture to become too smooth.

3 Check and adjust the seasoning, if necessary, then scrape the pâté into a serving dish. Swirl the top and chill lightly in the refrigerator. Serve the pâté sprinkled with parsley and paprika.

Cook's Tips
• *Conventional Worcestershire sauce is off-limits for vegetarians, as it contains anchovies. Look for the vegetarian version of this popular sauce. It is available in health-food stores.*
• *For extra flavour, add 15g/½oz dried porcini mushrooms, soaked in hot water for 30 minutes. Substitute 30ml/2 tbsp of the strained soaking water for the plain water.*

Roast Garlic & Goat's Cheese Pâté

The flavour of mellow roasted garlic goes well with this classic goat's cheese, walnut and herb pâté.

Serves 2–4

4 large garlic bulbs
4 fresh rosemary sprigs
8 fresh thyme sprigs
60ml/4 tbsp extra virgin olive oil
salt and ground black pepper

For the pâté

175g/6oz soft goat's cheese
5ml/1 tsp finely chopped fresh thyme
15ml/1 tbsp chopped fresh parsley
50g/2oz/ ½ cup shelled walnuts, chopped
15ml/1 tbsp walnut oil (optional)

To serve

4–8 slices sourdough bread
shelled walnuts
sea salt

1 Preheat the oven to 180°C/350°F/Gas 4. Strip the papery skin from the garlic bulbs. Place them in an ovenproof dish large enough to hold them snugly.

2 Tuck in the rosemary and thyme, drizzle the oil over and season to taste with salt and pepper. Cover the dish closely with foil and bake for 50–60 minutes, basting once. Remove from the oven and leave to cool.

3 Make the pâté. Cream the cheese with the thyme, parsley and chopped walnuts. Beat in 15ml/1 tbsp of the cooking oil from the garlic. Season to taste with salt and pepper, then transfer the pâté to a serving bowl.

4 Spread out the slices of sourdough bread in a grill (broiler) pan and brush them with the remaining cooking oil from the garlic. Grill (broil) until toasted.

5 If using the walnut oil, drizzle it over the goat's cheese pâté. Grind some black pepper over it. Place one or two bulbs of garlic on each plate and serve with the pâté and a couple of slices of toasted sourdough bread. Serve a few freshly shelled walnuts and a little sea salt with each portion.

Cheese Scrolls

Fascinating filo pastries with a feta and yogurt filling, Cheese Scrolls make very good snacks.

Makes 14–16

450g/1lb/2 cups feta cheese, well drained and finely crumbled
90ml/6 tbsp Greek (US strained plain) yogurt
2 eggs, beaten
14–16 sheets, 40 x 30cm/ 16 x 12in filo pastry, thawed if frozen
225g/8oz/1 cup butter, melted, plus extra for greasing
sea salt and chopped spring onions (scallions), for the topping

1 Preheat the oven to 200°C/400°F/Gas 6. In a large bowl combine the feta, yogurt and eggs, beating well until smooth.

2 Fit a piping (pastry) bag with a 1cm/ ½in plain round nozzle. Spoon half the cheese mixture into the bag.

3 Keeping the rest of the filo covered, lay one sheet on the work surface. Fold it in half to make a 30 x 20cm/12 x 8in rectangle, then brush with a little of the melted butter. Pipe a thick line of cheese mixture along one long edge, leaving a 5mm/ ¼in clear border.

4 Roll up the pastry to form a sausage shape, tucking in each end to prevent the filling from escaping. Brush with more melted butter. Form the "sausage" into a tight "S" or scroll-shape. Make more scrolls in the same way.

5 Arrange the scrolls on a buttered baking sheet and sprinkle with a little sea salt and chopped spring onion. Bake for about 20 minutes, or until crisp and golden brown. Cool on a wire rack before serving.

> **Cook's Tip**
> If you find it easier, you can shape the filled filo into crescents instead of scrolls.

Cheese Aigrettes

These choux buns, flavoured with mature Gruyère cheese and dusted with grated Parmesan, can be prepared ahead and deep-fried to serve.

Makes about 30

100g/3¾oz/scant 1 cup strong white bread flour
2.5ml/ ½ tsp paprika
2.5ml/ ½ tsp salt
75g/3oz/6 tbsp cold butter, diced
200ml/7fl oz/scant 1 cup water
3 eggs, beaten
75g/3oz/ ¾ cup coarsely grated mature (sharp) Gruyère cheese
vegetable oil, for deep-frying
50g/2oz piece of Parmesan cheese
ground black pepper
fresh flat leaf parsley sprigs, to garnish

1 Sift the flour, paprika and salt on to a sheet of greaseproof (waxed) paper. Add a generous grinding of black pepper.

2 Put the butter and water into a pan and heat gently. As soon as the butter has melted and the liquid starts to boil, tip in all the seasoned flour at once and beat vigorously with a wooden spoon until the dough comes away from the sides of the pan.

3 Remove the pan from the heat and set the paste aside to cool for about 5 minutes. Gradually beat in enough of the beaten eggs to give a stiff dropping consistency. Add the grated Gruyère and mix well.

4 Heat the oil for deep-frying to 180°C/350°F or until a cube of day-old bread turns golden brown in 60 seconds. Take a teaspoonful of the choux paste and use a second spoon to slide it into the hot oil. Make more aigrettes in the same way, but don't overcrowd the pan. Fry for 3–4 minutes, until golden brown. Remove with a slotted spoon and drain the aigrettes thoroughly on kitchen paper. Keep warm while you are cooking successive batches.

5 To serve, pile the aigrettes on a warmed serving dish, grate Parmesan over the top and garnish with fresh parsley sprigs. Serve immediately while hot.

Artichoke Rice Cakes with Melting Manchego

Cold cooked rice is very easy to mould. Shape it into balls, fill the centres with diced cheese and deep-fry to make a delectable snack.

Makes about 12 cakes
1 globe artichoke
50g/2oz/ ¼ cup butter
1 small onion, finely chopped
1 garlic clove, finely chopped

115g/4oz/ ⅔ cup risotto rice
450ml/ ¾ pint/scant 2 cups hot vegetable stock
50g/2oz/ ⅔ cup freshly grated Parmesan cheese
150g/5oz Manchego cheese, very finely diced
45–60ml/3–4 tbsp fine cornmeal
olive oil, for frying
salt and ground black pepper
flat leaf parsley, to garnish

1 Remove the stalk, leaves and choke to leave just the heart of the artichoke. Chop the heart finely. Melt the butter in a pan, add the artichoke heart, onion and garlic and cook over a low heat for 5 minutes, until softened. Stir in the rice and cook for about1 minute.

2 Add the stock a little at a time, stirring constantly and waiting until each addition has been absorbed before adding more.

3 After about 20 minutes the rice will be tender, but still firm at the centre of the grain, and all the liquid will have been absorbed. Season well, then stir in the Parmesan. Transfer to a bowl. Leave to cool, then cover and chill for at least 2 hours.

4 Spoon about 15ml/1 tbsp of the rice mixture into the palm of one hand, flatten slightly and place a few pieces of diced Manchego in the centre. Shape the rice around the cheese to make a small ball. Flatten slightly, then roll in the cornmeal, shaking off any excess. Repeat with the remaining mixture to make about 12 cakes.

5 Fry in hot olive oil for 4–5 minutes, until the rice cakes are crisp and golden brown. Drain on kitchen paper and serve hot, garnished with flat leaf parsley.

Wild Mushroom Pancakes with Chive Butter

Scotch pancakes are easy to make and taste wonderful with wild mushrooms. The unusual hedgehog fungus has been used here, but any wild or cultivated mushrooms could be used instead.

Makes 12 pancakes
350g/12oz/about 5 cups hedgehog fungus or other wild mushrooms

50g/2oz/ ¼ cup butter
175g/6oz/1 ½ cups self-raising (self-rising) flour
2 eggs
200ml/7fl oz/scant 1 cup milk
salt and ground white pepper

For the chive butter
15g/ ½ oz/scant 1 cup fresh finely chopped chives
115g/4oz/ ½ cup butter, softened
5ml/1 tsp lemon juice

1 First make the chive butter by mixing all the ingredients together. Turn out on to a 25cm/10in square of greaseproof (waxed) paper and form into a sausage. Roll up, twist both ends of the paper and chill for about 1 hour, until firm.

2 Slice one-quarter of the mushrooms and set them aside. Finely chop the remaining mushrooms. Melt half the butter in a frying pan and cook the chopped mushrooms until soft and all the moisture has evaporated. Spread them on a tray and leave to cool. Cook the sliced mushrooms in a knob (pat) of butter.

3 Sift the flour into a bowl and season with salt and pepper. Beat the eggs with the milk in a jug (pitcher). Add to the flour, stirring to make a thick batter. Add the chopped mushrooms.

4 Heat the remaining butter in the clean frying pan. Arrange small heaps of sliced mushrooms on the base of the pan, using five mushroom slices each time, then pour a little batter over each heap to make 5cm/2in Scotch pancakes.

5 When bubbles appear on the surface, turn the pancakes over and cook for a further 10–15 seconds. Serve warm with slices of the chive butter.

Fontina Pan Bagna

When the weather is hot, a crusty flute or baguette filled with juicy tomatoes, crisp red onion, green pepper, thinly sliced Fontina cheese and sliced black olives makes a refreshing and substantial snack.

Serves 2–4
1 small red onion, thinly sliced
1 fresh flute or baguette
extra virgin olive oil
3 ripe plum tomatoes, thinly sliced
1 small green (bell) pepper, halved, seeded and thinly sliced
200g/7oz Fontina cheese, thinly sliced
about 12 pitted black olives, sliced
a handful of fresh flat leaf parsley or basil leaves
salt and ground black pepper
fresh basil sprigs, to garnish

1 Soak the slices of red onion in plenty of cold water for at least 1 hour, then drain well in a colander, tip on to kitchen paper and pat dry.

2 Slice the flute or baguette in half lengthways and brush the cut sides well with olive oil. Lay the tomato slices down one side and season well with salt and black pepper.

3 Top with the green pepper slices, then add the onion slices. Arrange the cheese and olives on top. Sprinkle over the parsley or basil leaves and season with salt and pepper again.

4 Press the halves together, then wrap the filled loaf tightly in clear film (plastic wrap) to compress it. Chill for at least 1 hour. Unwrap and cut diagonally into thick slices. Garnish with basil sprigs and serve immediately.

> **Cook's Tips**
> • *This is a good choice for a picnic. Pack the loaf, uncut and still wrapped in clear film (plastic wrap), and cut into slices just before serving. Do not forget to take a sharp knife with you.*
> • *Other springy-textured cheeses, such as Taleggio and Havarti, could be used instead of Fontina.*

Four Cheese Ciabatta Pizzas

Few dishes are as simple – or as satisfying – as this pizza made by topping a halved loaf of ciabatta.

Serves 2
1 loaf of ciabatta
1 garlic clove, halved
30–45ml/2–3 tbsp olive oil
about 90ml/6 tbsp passata (bottled strained tomatoes)
1 small red onion, thinly sliced
30ml/2 tbsp chopped pitted black olives
about 50g/2oz each of four cheeses, one mature (sharp) (Parmesan or Cheddar), one blue-veined (Gorgonzola or Stilton), one mild (Fontina or Emmenthal) and a goat's cheese, sliced, grated or crumbled
pine nuts or cumin seeds, to sprinkle
salt and ground black pepper
fresh basil sprigs, to garnish

1 Preheat the oven to 200°C/400°F/Gas 6. Split the ciabatta loaf in half. Rub the cut sides with the cut sides of the garlic clove, then brush over the olive oil.

2 Spread the passata evenly over the ciabatta halves. Separate the onion slices into rings and arrange them on each cut loaf, with the chopped olives on top. Season generously with salt and pepper.

3 Divide the cheeses equally among the ciabatta halves and then sprinkle the pine nuts or cumin seeds over the top.

4 Bake for 10–12 minutes, until the cheese topping is bubbling and golden brown. Cut the ciabatta pizzas into slices and serve immediately, garnished with basil sprigs.

> **Cook's Tip**
> *Passata (bottled strained tomatoes) is a very useful ingredient to keep in the store cupboard (pantry). Strained tomato pulp with an intense flavour, it comes in jars, cans and cartons and is widely available. Sugocasa can be used instead.*

Layered Vegetable Terrine

With its jacket of green, this spinach, pepper and potato terrine looks very pretty.

Serves 6
3 red (bell) peppers, halved
    and seeded
450g/1lb waxy potatoes, halved
1 medium courgette (zucchini),
    sliced lengthways
115g/4oz spinach
    leaves, trimmed
25g/1oz/2 tbsp butter
pinch of freshly grated nutmeg
115g/4oz/1 cup grated
    Cheddar cheese
salt and ground black pepper
torn lettuce leaves and tomato
    wedges, to serve

1 Place the pepper halves, skin side up, on a grill (broiler) rack and grill (broil) until the skins have charred. Transfer to a bowl, cover with crumpled kitchen paper and leave to cool.

2 Meanwhile, bring a pan of lightly salted water to the boil. Cook the potatoes for 15 minutes. Drain and set aside. Bring a separate pan of water to the boil and add the courgette slices. Blanch them for 1 minute, then lift out with a slotted spoon. Add the spinach to the boiling water, blanch for a few seconds, then drain and pat dry on kitchen paper.

3 Preheat the oven to 180°C/350°F/Gas 4. Line the base and sides of a 900g/2lb loaf tin (pan) with the spinach, overlapping the leaves slightly. Slice the potatoes thinly. Lay one-third of them in the base of the tin, dot with a little butter and season with salt, pepper and nutmeg. Sprinkle some cheese over.

4 Peel the red peppers. Arrange half of them on top of the potatoes. Sprinkle with a little cheese and add a layer of courgettes. Lay a further third of the potatoes on top with the remaining peppers and more cheese, seasoning as you go. Top with the final layer of potatoes and sprinkle over any remaining cheese. Fold the spinach leaves over. Cover with foil.

5 Place the loaf tin in a roasting pan and pour in boiling water to come halfway up the sides. Bake for about 1 hour. Turn out the terrine and serve sliced, with lettuce and tomatoes.

Courgette, Mushroom & Pesto Panino

Packed with delectable vegetables, cheese and pesto, this picnic loaf is certain to impress. It is easy to transport, slices beautifully and tastes very good indeed.

Serves 6
1 medium country-style loaf
30ml/2 tbsp olive oil
3 courgettes (zucchini),
    sliced lengthways
250g/9oz/3½ cups brown cap
    (cremini) mushrooms, sliced
1 garlic clove, chopped
5ml/1 tsp dried oregano
45ml/3 tbsp pesto
250g/9oz Taleggio cheese, sliced
50g/2oz/2 cups green
    salad leaves
salt and ground black pepper

1 Slice off the top third of the loaf and invert it on a board. Remove most of the crumb from the inside of both the lid and base, leaving a shell about 1cm/½in thick.

2 Brush a ridged griddle pan with oil and cook the courgettes until they are tender and browned.

3 Meanwhile, heat the remaining oil in a frying pan and cook the mushrooms, garlic and oregano for 3 minutes. Season well.

4 Arrange half the courgettes in the base of the hollow loaf, then spread with half the pesto. Top with half the cheese and salad leaves and all the mushroom mixture. Add one more layer each of the remaining cheese, salad leaves and courgettes. Spread the rest of the pesto over the inside of the bread lid and place it on top.

5 Press the lid down gently, wrap the loaf in clear film (plastic wrap) and leave to cool. Chill overnight. Serve cut into wedges.

Cook's Tip
The courgettes (zucchini) can be grilled (broiled) conventionally.

Cannellini Bean & Rosemary Bruschetta

More brunch than breakfast, this dish is a sophisticated version of beans on toast.

Serves 4
150g/5oz/ ⅔ cup dried
  cannellini beans
5 tomatoes
45ml/3 tbsp olive oil, plus extra
  for drizzling
2 sun-dried tomatoes in oil,
  drained and finely chopped

1 garlic clove, crushed
30ml/2 tbsp chopped
  fresh rosemary
salt and ground black pepper
a handful of fresh basil leaves,
  to garnish

To serve
8 slices Italian-style bread, such as
  ciabatta
1 large garlic clove, halved

1 Place the beans in a large bowl and cover with water. Leave to soak overnight. Drain and rinse the beans, then place in a pan and cover with fresh water. Bring to the boil and boil rapidly for 10 minutes. Reduce the heat and simmer for 50–60 minutes, or until tender. Drain and set aside.

2 Meanwhile, place the tomatoes in a bowl, cover with boiling water and leave for 30 seconds. Remove with a slotted spoon, then peel, seed and chop the flesh.

3 Heat the oil in a frying pan, add the fresh and sun-dried tomatoes, garlic and rosemary. Cook over a medium heat, stirring occasionally, for 2 minutes, until the tomatoes begin to break down and soften.

4 Add the tomato mixture to the cannellini beans, season to taste with salt and pepper and mix well. Keep warm.

5 When ready to serve, rub both sides of the bread slices with the cut sides of the garlic clove, then toast lightly. Spoon the cannellini bean and tomato mixture on top of the toast. Sprinkle with fresh basil leaves and drizzle with a little extra olive oil before serving.

Goat's Cheese & Gin Crostini

A gin marinade accentuates the flavour of goat's cheese, which melts beautifully over the spring onions on these tasty toasts.

Serves 4
8 slices chèvre
15ml/1 tbsp gin
30ml/2 tbsp walnut oil
30ml/2 tbsp olive oil
4 slices Italian or French bread

1 garlic clove, halved
2 spring onions (scallions), sliced
6 walnut halves, coarsely broken
15ml/1 tbsp chopped
  fresh parsley
ground black pepper
cherry tomatoes and mixed salad
  leaves, to garnish
Orange and Tomato Salsa,
  to serve

1 Spread out the cheese slices in a single layer in a shallow bowl. Pour over the gin, walnut oil and olive oil, then cover and leave in a cool place to marinate for 1 hour.

2 Put the slices of bread on a grill (broiler) rack. Toast them under a hot grill on one side, then turn them over and rub the untoasted surfaces with the cut pieces of garlic. Brush with a little of the marinade used for the goat's cheese, then sprinkle over the sliced spring onions. Top with the slices of cheese.

3 Pour over any remaining marinade, season with pepper and cook the crostini under a hot grill until the cheese has melted and browned. Sprinkle over the walnuts and parsley. Garnish with the tomatoes and salad leaves and serve with the salsa.

> **Cook's Tip**
> Chèvre is French goat's milk cheese. It is often cylindrical in shape, which makes it perfect for this dish. Use a natural-rind cheese with a firm, but not hard texture. Do not let it get wet in storage, as this will spoil it.

Orange & Tomato Salsa

Fruity, but not too sweet, this salsa is the perfect accompaniment for the crostini. It also tastes wonderful with Lancashire or Cheddar cheese and French bread as part of a bread and cheese lunch.

Serves 4
2 oranges
5 tomatoes, peeled, seeded
  and chopped
15ml/1 tbsp shredded fresh basil
30ml/2 tbsp olive oil
pinch of soft light brown sugar
fresh basil sprig, to garnish

1 Cut a slice off the top and bottom of each orange. Place each orange in turn on a board and cut off the skin, taking care to remove all the bitter white pith. Working over a bowl to catch the juices, cut between the membranes to release the segments.
2 Add the segments to the bowl, with the tomatoes, shredded basil, olive oil and brown sugar. Mix well. Serve at room temperature, garnished with the basil.

Eggs Benedict with Quick Hollandaise

This classic American brunch dish originated in New York, and is ideal for serving on a special occasion, such as a birthday treat or New Year's day.

Serves 4
4 large (US extra large) eggs, plus
  2 egg yolks
5ml/1 tsp mustard powder
15ml/1 tbsp white wine vinegar
  or lemon juice
175g/6oz/¾ cup butter, plus
  extra for spreading
4 muffins, split
30ml/2 tbsp rinsed capers
salt and ground black pepper
a little chopped fresh parsley,
  to garnish

1 Put the egg yolks in a blender or food processor. Add the mustard and a pinch of salt and pepper and process for a few seconds. Add the vinegar or lemon juice and process again.

2 Heat the butter until it is on the point of bubbling, then, with the motor running, slowly pour it through the lid or feeder tube. When the mixture is thick and creamy, switch off the blender or food processor and set the sauce aside.

3 Toast the split muffins under a hot grill. Cut four of the halves in two and butter them lightly. Place the four uncut halves on warmed plates and leave unbuttered.

4 Poach the eggs either in gently simmering water or in an egg poacher. Drain well and slip carefully on to the muffin halves. Spoon the hollandaise sauce over the muffins, then sprinkle with capers and parsley. Serve immediately with the buttered muffin quarters.

> **Variation**
> *Instead of the toasted muffin, you could make more of a main meal by serving the poached eggs and sauce on a bed of lightly steamed or blanched spinach.*

Mixed Pepper Pipérade

Every cook needs recipes like this one. Nourishing, tasty and made in moments, Pipérade is based on everyday ingredients.

Serves 4
30ml/2 tbsp olive oil
1 onion, chopped
1 red (bell) pepper
1 green (bell) pepper
4 tomatoes, peeled and chopped
1 garlic clove, crushed
4 large (US extra large) eggs,
  beaten with 15ml/1 tbsp water
4 large, thick slices of wholemeal
  (whole-wheat) bread
butter, for spreading (optional)
ground black pepper
fresh herbs, to garnish

1 Heat the oil in a large frying pan. Add the onion and cook over a low heat, stirring occasionally, for 5 minutes, until it has softened but not browned.

2 Cut the peppers in half, remove the seeds and slice the flesh thinly. Stir the pepper slices into the onion and cook gently for about 5 minutes.

3 Stir in the tomatoes and garlic, season generously with black pepper and cook for 5 minutes more.

4 Pour the egg mixture over the vegetables and cook for 2–3 minutes, stirring occasionally, until the pipérade has thickened to the consistency of lightly scrambled eggs.

5 While the egg mixture is cooking, toast the bread. Butter it, if you like, and serve the toast and pipérade on individual plates, garnished with fresh herbs.

> **Cook's Tip**
> *Choose eggs that have been date-stamped to be sure that they are fresh. Do not stir the pipérade too much or the eggs may become unpleasantly rubbery.*

Mozzarella in Carozza with Fresh Tomato Salsa

These upmarket toasted sandwiches come from Italy. After being filled, they are dipped in beaten egg and fried like French toast.

Serves 4
200g/7oz mozzarella cheese,
 thinly sliced
8 thin slices of bread,
 crusts removed
pinch of dried oregano
30ml/2 tbsp freshly grated
 Parmesan cheese

3 eggs, beaten
olive oil, for frying
salt and ground black pepper
fresh herbs, to garnish

For the salsa
4 ripe plum tomatoes, peeled,
 seeded and finely chopped
15ml/1 tbsp chopped
 fresh parsley
5ml/1 tsp balsamic vinegar
15ml/1 tbsp extra virgin olive oil

1 Arrange the mozzarella on four slices of the bread. Season with salt and pepper and sprinkle with a little dried oregano and the Parmesan. Top with the other bread slices and press them firmly together.

2 Pour the beaten eggs into a large shallow dish and season with salt and pepper. Add the cheese sandwiches, two at a time, pressing them into the eggs with a fish slice or metal spatula until they are well coated. Repeat with the remaining sandwiches, then leave them to stand for 10 minutes.

3 Meanwhile, make the salsa. Put the chopped tomatoes in a bowl and add the parsley. Stir in the balsamic vinegar and the extra virgin olive oil. Season to taste with salt and pepper and set aside.

4 Pour olive oil to a depth of 5mm/¼in into a large frying pan. When it is hot, add the sandwiches carefully, in batches, and cook for about 2 minutes on each side, until golden and crisp. Drain well on kitchen paper. Cut in half. Serve on individual plates, garnished with fresh herbs and accompanied by the salsa.

Chive Scrambled Eggs in Brioches

Lift the lid on baked brioches and discover a glorious mixture of creamy scrambled egg and fried brown cap mushrooms.

Serves 4
115g/4oz/½ cup butter
75g/3oz/generous 1 cup brown
 cap (cremini) mushrooms, finely
 sliced
4 individual brioches
8 eggs, lightly mixed
15ml/1 tbsp chopped fresh
 chives, plus extra to garnish
salt and ground black pepper

1 Preheat the oven to 180°C/350°F/Gas 4. Melt one-quarter of the butter in a frying pan. Cook the mushrooms for about 3 minutes, or until soft, then set aside and keep warm.

2 Slice the tops off the brioches, then scoop out the centres and save them for breadcrumbs. Put the brioches and lids on a baking sheet and bake for 5 minutes, until hot and slightly crisp.

3 Meanwhile, beat the eggs lightly and season to taste. Heat the remaining butter in a heavy pan over a gentle heat.

4 Add the eggs. Using a wooden spoon, stir constantly until about three-quarters of the egg is semi-solid and creamy – this should take 2–3 minutes. Remove the pan from the heat and stir in the chopped chives.

5 Immediately spoon one-quarter of the fried mushrooms into the base of each brioche and top with the scrambled eggs, divided equally among them. Sprinkle with extra chives, balance the brioche lids on top and serve immediately.

Cook's Tip
Timing and temperature are crucial for perfect scrambled eggs. When cooked for too long over too high heat, eggs become dry and crumbly; undercooked eggs are sloppy and unappealing.

Indian Potato Pancakes

Although described as pancakes, these classic, crisp cakes are more like bhajis. They are ideal as part of a curry supper.

Makes 10
2 potatoes, about 300g/11oz
    total weight
2.5ml/1½ tsp garam masala or
    curry powder
4 spring onions (scallions),
    finely chopped
1 large (US extra large) egg
    white, lightly beaten
30ml/2 tbsp vegetable oil
salt and ground black pepper
chutney and relishes, to serve

1 Peel the potatoes, then grate them into a large bowl. Taking a handful at a time, squeeze out the excess liquid, then pat the potatoes dry with kitchen paper and put them in a separate medium bowl.

2 Add the garam masala or curry powder, spring onions and egg white to the potatoes. Stir to combine, then season to taste with salt and pepper.

3 Heat the oil in a non-stick frying pan over a medium heat. Taking care not to overcrowd the pan, drop tablespoonfuls of the batter on to the surface and flatten each to a pancake with the back of the spoon.

4 Cook for a few minutes and then flip each pancake over. Cook for 3 minutes more.

5 Drain on kitchen paper and keep hot while cooking more pancakes in the same way. Serve hot, with chutney and relishes.

Cook's Tips
• Grate the potatoes at the last minute, as the flesh will turn brown if they are left standing.
• Garam masala is a mixture of spices that usually includes dried chilli, cinnamon, curry leaves, coriander, cumin, mustard and fenugreek seeds, and black peppercorns.

Baked Eggs en Cocotte with Wild Mushrooms & Chives

These simple, but utterly delicious baked eggs, served with toast, make a splendid light meal.

Serves 6
65g/2½oz/5 tbsp butter
2 shallots, finely chopped
1 small garlic clove,
    finely chopped
250g/9oz/3 cups wild
    mushrooms, finely chopped
15ml/1 tbsp lemon juice
5ml/1 tsp chopped fresh tarragon
30ml/2 tbsp crème fraîche
30ml/2 tbsp chopped fresh chives
6 eggs
salt and ground black pepper
whole chives, to garnish
buttered toast, to serve

1 Melt 50g/2oz/4 tbsp of the butter in a frying pan and cook the shallots and garlic until softened but not browned.

2 Increase the heat and add the mushrooms, then cook briskly, stirring frequently, until the mushrooms lose their moisture and are just starting to brown slightly.

3 Stir in the lemon juice and tarragon and continue to cook, stirring occasionally, until the mushrooms have absorbed the liquid. Stir in half the crème fraîche and half the chopped chives and season to taste with salt and pepper.

4 Preheat the oven to 190°C/375°F/Gas 5. Distribute the mushroom mixture equally among six ramekins. Sprinkle the remaining chopped chives over the mushrooms.

5 Break an egg into each dish, add a dab of crème fraîche and season to taste with pepper. Dot with the remaining butter. Bake for 10–15 minutes, or until the whites of the eggs are set and the yolks cooked to your liking.

6 Serve immediately, garnished with the fresh chives and accompanied by lots of hot, buttered toast.

Baked Eggs with Double Cream

This rich dish is very easy and quick to make.

Serves 4
15g/½oz/1 tbsp unsalted (sweet)
    butter, softened, for greasing
120ml/4fl oz/½ cup double
    (heavy) cream
30ml/2 tbsp chopped fresh chives
4 eggs
115g/4oz/1 cup finely grated
    Gruyère cheese
salt and ground black pepper

1 Preheat the oven to 180°C/350°F/Gas 4. Grease four individual gratin dishes. Mix the cream with the chives, and season to taste with salt and pepper.
2 Break an egg into each dish and top with the cream mixture. Sprinkle the cheese around the edge of each dish. Bake for 15–20 minutes. When cooked, brown the tops briefly under a hot grill (broiler), then serve.

Thai Tempeh Cakes with Sweet Dipping Sauce

Made from soya beans, tempeh is similar to tofu, but has a nuttier taste. Here, it is combined with spices and formed into small patties.

Makes 8 cakes
1 lemon grass stalk, outer leaves removed, coarsely chopped
2 garlic cloves, chopped
2 spring onions (scallions), finely chopped
2 shallots, coarsely chopped
2 fresh chillies, seeded and coarsely chopped
2.5cm/1in piece of fresh root ginger, finely chopped
60ml/4 tbsp chopped fresh coriander (cilantro), plus extra to garnish
250g/9oz tempeh, thawed if frozen, sliced
15ml/1 tbsp freshly squeezed lime juice
5ml/1 tsp caster (superfine) sugar
45ml/3 tbsp plain (all-purpose) flour
1 large (US extra large) egg, lightly beaten
vegetable oil, for frying
salt and ground black pepper

For the dipping sauce
45ml/3 tbsp mirin
45ml/3 tbsp white wine vinegar
2 spring onions (scallions), thinly sliced
15ml/1 tbsp granulated sugar
2 fresh red chillies, chopped
30ml/2 tbsp chopped fresh coriander (cilantro)

1 To make the dipping sauce, mix together all the ingredients with a large pinch of salt in a small bowl and set aside.

2 Place the lemon grass, garlic, spring onions, shallots, chillies, ginger and coriander in a food processor or blender and process to a coarse paste.

3 Add the tempeh, lime juice and sugar, then process until thoroughly combined. Add the flour and egg and season with salt and pepper. Process again to a coarse, sticky paste.

4 Using a tablespoon, scoop up a generous quantity of the tempeh mixture. Dampen your hands, then shape the mixture to a round, slightly flattened cake. Make seven more tempeh cakes in the same way.

5 Heat enough oil to cover the base of a large frying pan. Cook the cakes, in batches, for 5–6 minutes, turning once, until golden. Drain on kitchen paper. Serve warm with the dipping sauce, garnished with the reserved coriander.

> **Cook's Tip**
> *Use red or green chillies, choosing a variety with the degree of fieriness you require. In general, dark green chillies tend to be hotter than pale green ones, which, in turn, are hotter than red chillies. (As the chillies ripen, they become red and relatively sweeter.) Also, the small, pointed chillies tend to be fiercer than the larger, rounder ones. However, there are always exceptions and even different pods from the same plant can vary in their level of spiciness. Err on the side of caution, if in doubt.*

Courgette Fritters with Chilli Jam

Rather like a thick chutney, chilli jam is hot, sweet and sticky. It adds a piquancy to these light courgette fritters but is also delicious with pies or a chunk of cheese.

Makes 12 fritters
450g/1lb courgettes (zucchini)
50g/2oz/ 2⁄3 cup freshly grated Parmesan cheese
2 eggs, beaten
60ml/4 tbsp unbleached plain (all-purpose) flour
vegetable oil, for frying
salt and ground black pepper

For the chilli jam
75ml/5 tbsp olive oil
4 large onions, diced
4 garlic cloves, chopped
1–2 fresh Thai chillies, seeded and sliced
25g/1oz/2 tbsp soft dark brown sugar
a few thin slices of fresh red chilli, to garnish

1 First make the chilli jam. Heat the oil in a frying pan, add the onions and garlic, then lower the heat and cook the mixture, stirring frequently, for 20 minutes, until the onions are very soft.

2 Leave the onion mixture to cool, then put it into a food processor or blender. Add the Thai red chillies and brown sugar and process until smooth, then return the mixture to the pan. Cook over a low heat, stirring frequently, for about 10 minutes, or until the liquid evaporates and the mixture has the consistency of jam. Cool slightly.

3 To make the fritters, grate the courgettes coarsely on to a clean dishtowel, then gather up the sides and squeeze tightly to remove any excess moisture. Tip the courgettes into a bowl and stir in the grated Parmesan, eggs and flour and season to taste with salt and pepper.

4 Heat enough vegetable oil to cover the base of a large frying pan. Add 30ml/2 tbsp of the mixture for each fritter and cook three fritters at a time. Cook for 2–3 minutes on each side, until golden, then keep warm while you cook the remaining fritters. Drain on kitchen paper and serve hot with a spoonful of the chilli jam, garnished with a slice of chilli.

Wild Mushroom Gratin with Beaufort Cheese, New Potatoes & Walnuts

This is one of the simplest and most delicious ways of cooking mushrooms. Serve this dish as the Swiss do, with gherkins.

Serves 4
900g/2lb small new or
   salad potatoes
50g/2oz/ ¼ cup butter or 60ml/
   4 tbsp olive oil
350g/12oz/4½ cups assorted
   wild and cultivated mushrooms,
   thinly sliced

175g/6oz Beaufort or Fontina
   cheese, thinly sliced
50g/2oz/ ½ cup broken
   walnuts, toasted
salt and ground black pepper
fresh flat leaf parsley, coarsely
   chopped, to garnish
12 gherkins, sliced, to serve

1 Bring a large pan of lightly salted water to the boil over a medium heat and cook the potatoes for about 20 minutes, until tender. Drain well and return them to the pan. Add a knob (pat) of butter or a splash of oil and cover to keep warm.

2 Heat the remaining butter or olive oil in a heavy frying pan that can safely be used under the grill (broiler). (Cover a wooden handle with foil to protect it.) Add the sliced mushrooms and cook over a low heat, stirring occasionally, until their juices begin to run, then increase the heat and cook until most of the juices have been absorbed again. Season to taste with salt and pepper.

3 Meanwhile, preheat the grill. Arrange the slices of cheese on top of the mushrooms. Place the pan under the grill and cook until the cheese is bubbly and golden brown.

4 Sprinkle with the toasted walnuts, garnish with parsley and serve with the buttered potatoes and sliced gherkins.

Courgette Fritters with Pistou

The sauce is the French equivalent of pesto. It provides a lovely contrast to these delicious fritters.

Serves 4
450g/1lb courgettes
   (zucchini), trimmed
75g/3oz/ ¾ cup plain (all-
   purpose) flour
1 egg, separated
15ml/1 tbsp olive oil

75ml/5 tbsp water
vegetable oil, for frying
salt and ground black pepper

For the pistou
15g/ ½ oz/ ½ cup fresh
   basil leaves
4 garlic cloves, coarsely chopped
75g/3oz/1 cup freshly grated
   Parmesan cheese
finely grated rind of 1 lemon
150ml/ ¼ pint/ ⅔ cup olive oil

1 Start by making the pistou. Put the basil leaves and garlic in a mortar and crush with a pestle to a fairly fine paste. Work in the grated Parmesan and lemon rind. Gradually blend in the olive oil, a little at a time, until fully incorporated, then transfer the pistou to a small serving dish.

2 Grate the courgettes into a sieve. Sprinkle with plenty of salt. Place the sieve over a bowl, leave for 1 hour, then rinse thoroughly. Drain, then dry well on kitchen paper.

3 Sift the flour into a bowl and make a well in the centre, then add the egg yolk, olive oil and water to the well. Whisk, gradually incorporating the surrounding flour to make a smooth batter. Season to taste with salt and pepper and set aside to rest for 30 minutes.

4 Stir the courgettes into the batter. Whisk the egg white until stiff, then fold it into the batter.

5 Heat the vegetable oil in a large, heavy frying pan. Add tablespoons of batter to the oil and cook for about 2 minutes, until golden. Lift the fritters out with a fish slice or metal spatula and drain well on kitchen paper. Keep warm while you are cooking the remainder. Transfer to warm plates and serve immediately with the sauce.

Hot Halloumi with Roasted Peppers

Salty and full of flavour, Halloumi cheese takes on a wonderful texture when grilled or fried. A tumble of roasted sweet peppers makes an especially fine accompaniment.

Serves 4

6 (bell) peppers of mixed colours, halved and seeded
olive oil
30ml/2 tbsp balsamic vinegar
small handful of raisins (optional)
300g/11oz Halloumi cheese, thickly sliced
salt and ground black pepper
flat leaf parsley, to garnish

1 Place the pepper halves, skin side up, on a grill (broiler) rack and grill (broil) until the skins have blistered and charred. Transfer to a bowl and cover with crumpled kitchen paper. Leave to cool slightly, then peel off the skins. Slice the flesh into a bowl. Save any juices and mix these with the peppers.

2 Pour a little olive oil over the peppers. Add the vinegar and raisins, if using, and season with salt and pepper to taste. Toss lightly and leave to cool.

3 When ready to serve, divide the pepper salad among four plates. In a large, heavy frying pan heat olive oil to a depth of about 5mm/¼in. Fry the Halloumi slices over a medium-high heat for 2–3 minutes, or until golden brown on both sides, turning them halfway through cooking.

4 Drain the Halloumi thoroughly on kitchen paper and serve with the roasted peppers and a parsley garnish.

> **Cook's Tips**
> • For a crisp coating on the Halloumi, toss the slices in plain (all-purpose) flour before frying them.
> • Halloumi can be grilled (broiled) or griddled instead of fried. Preheat a grill (broiler) or ridged griddling pan, add the cheese and cook until golden brown, turning once.

Malfatti with Roasted Pepper Sauce

Deliciously light spinach dumplings are wonderful with a smoky sauce.

Serves 5

500g/1¼lb fresh leaf spinach
1 onion, finely chopped
1 garlic clove, crushed
15ml/1 tbsp extra virgin olive oil
350g/12oz/1½ cups ricotta cheese
3 eggs, beaten
50g/2oz/½ cup natural-coloured dried breadcrumbs
50g/2oz/½ cup plain (all-purpose) flour
50g/2oz/⅔ cup freshly grated Parmesan cheese
freshly grated nutmeg
25g/1oz/2 tbsp butter, melted
salt and ground black pepper

For the sauce
2 red (bell) peppers, quartered and seeded
30ml/2 tbsp extra virgin olive oil
1 onion, chopped
400g/14oz can chopped tomatoes
150ml/¼ pint/⅔ cup water

1 Make the sauce. Grill (broil) the peppers, skin side up, until charred. Place in a bowl, cover with crumpled kitchen paper and leave to cool. Peel off the skins and chop the flesh.

2 Heat the oil in a pan and cook the onion and peppers for 5 minutes. Add the tomatoes and water and season. Bring to the boil, lower the heat and simmer for 15 minutes. Process in a food processor or blender, then return to the clean pan.

3 Trim any thick stalks from the spinach, then blanch in a pan of boiling water for about 1 minute. Drain, refresh under cold water and drain again. Squeeze dry, then chop finely. Put the onion, garlic, oil, ricotta, eggs, breadcrumbs and spinach in a bowl. Mix well, then stir in the flour and 5ml/1 tsp salt. Add half the Parmesan, then season to taste with pepper and nutmeg. Roll the mixture into 15 small logs and chill lightly.

4 Bring a pan of water to the boil. Cook the malfatti, in batches, for 5 minutes. Remove and toss them with the melted butter. Reheat the sauce and divide it among five plates. Arrange three malfatti on each and sprinkle over the remaining Parmesan.

Fonduta

Fondues are coming back into fashion. They are lots of fun and just perfect for casual entertaining. This variation is rich and tasty.

Serves 4
250g/9oz Fontina or Gruyère cheese, diced
250ml/8fl oz/1 cup milk
15g/½oz/1 tbsp butter
2 eggs, lightly beaten
ground black pepper
1 loaf ciabatta or focaccia, cut in large cubes, to serve

1 Put the cheese in a bowl, pour over the milk and leave to soak for 2–3 hours. Transfer to a double boiler or a heatproof bowl set over a pan of simmering water.

2 Add the butter and eggs and cook gently, stirring until the cheese has melted and the sauce is smooth and thick, with the consistency of custard. Remove from the heat and season to taste with pepper. Transfer to a serving dish and serve immediately with the bread.

Dutch Fondue

This is an amazingly easy, yet delicious lunch dish.

Serves 4
250ml/8fl oz/1 cup white wine
15 ml/1 tbsp lemon juice
450g/1lb Gouda cheese, grated
15 ml/1 tbsp cornflour (cornstarch)
30 ml/2 tbsp water
30 ml/2 tbsp gin
ground black pepper
vegetable crudités and bread cubes, to serve

1 Bring the wine and lemon juice to the boil in a pan over a low heat. Gradually stir in the cheese until melted.
2 Mix the cornflour and water to a paste and stir into the fondue. Bring to the boil, stirring constantly, add the gin and season with pepper.
3 Transfer to a fondue. Serve with the vegetables and bread.

Leek Soufflé

Some people think a soufflé is a rather tricky dish for entertaining, but it is really quite easy.

Serves 2–3
40g/1½oz/3 tbsp butter, plus extra for greasing
15ml/1 tbsp sunflower oil
2 leeks, thinly sliced
about 300ml/ ½ pint/ 1¼ cups milk
25g/oz/ ¼ cup plain (all-purpose) flour
4 eggs, separated
75g/3oz/ ¾ cup grated Gruyère or Emmenthal cheese
salt and ground black pepper

1 Preheat the oven to 180°C/350°F/Gas 4. Butter a 1.2 litre/ 2 pint/5 cup soufflé dish. Heat the oil and 15g/ ½oz/1 tbsp of the butter in a small pan and cook the leeks gently, stirring occasionally, for 4–5 minutes, until soft but not brown.

2 Stir in the milk and bring to the boil. Cover, then simmer for 4–5 minutes, until the leeks are tender. Drain, reserving the liquid. Set the leeks aside and strain the liquid. Measure and add extra milk to make it up to 300ml/ ½ pint/1¼ cups.

3 Melt the remaining butter in a pan, stir in the flour and cook for 1 minute. Gradually add the milk, whisking constantly until the mixture boils and thickens to a smooth sauce.

4 Remove it from the heat. Cool slightly, then beat in the egg yolks, cheese and reserved leeks. Season to taste.

5 Whisk the egg whites until stiff. Using a large metal spoon, fold them into the leek and egg mixture. Pour into the prepared soufflé dish and bake in the oven for about 30 minutes, until golden and puffy. Serve immediately.

Cook's Tip
Everything except whisking the egg whites can be done in advance. Finish making the soufflé when your guests arrive and half an hour later you'll be sitting down to a superb light meal.

Celeriac & Blue Cheese Roulade

Celeriac adds a subtle, but distinctive flavour to this attractive dish.

Serves 6
15g/½oz/1 tbsp butter
225g/8oz cooked spinach, drained and chopped
150ml/¼ pint/⅔ cup single (light) cream
4 large (US extra large) eggs, separated
60ml/4 tbsp freshly grated Parmesan cheese
pinch of freshly grated nutmeg
salt and ground black pepper

For the filling
1 large celeriac, about 225g/8oz
lemon juice, to taste
75g/3oz St Agur cheese
115g/4oz/½ cup fromage frais (farmer's cheese) or thick natural (plain) yogurt

1 Preheat the oven to 200°C/400°F/Gas 6. Line a 33 × 23cm/13 × 9in Swiss roll tin (jelly roll pan) with baking parchment or greaseproof (waxed) paper.

2 Melt the butter in a pan and add the spinach. Cook gently until all the liquid has evaporated, stirring frequently. Remove from the heat and stir in the cream, egg yolks, Parmesan and nutmeg. Season to taste with salt and pepper.

3 Whisk the egg whites until stiff, fold them gently into the spinach mixture and spoon into the prepared tin. Spread the mixture evenly and smooth the surface.

4 Bake for 10–15 minutes until the roulade is firm to the touch and lightly golden on top. Carefully turn out on to a sheet of baking parchment and peel away the lining. Roll it up with the paper inside and leave to cool slightly.

5 Make the filling. Peel the celeriac, grate it into a bowl and sprinkle well with lemon juice. Blend the blue cheese and fromage frais or yogurt together and mix with the celeriac. Season with a little black pepper.

6 Carefully unroll the roulade, spread the filling evenly over the surface and roll up again. Serve, cut into slices.

Twice-baked Spinach, Mushroom & Goat's Cheese Roulade

A roulade is really a Swiss roll soufflé. Because it has air trapped inside, it magically rises again on reheating and becomes quite crisp on the outside.

Serves 4
150g/5oz/⅔ cup butter, plus extra, for greasing
50g/2oz/½ cup plain (all-purpose) flour
300ml/½ pint/1¼ cups milk
100g/3¾oz chèvre (goat's cheese), chopped
40g/1½oz/½ cup freshly grated Parmesan cheese, plus extra for sprinkling
4 eggs, separated
225g/8oz/3 cups fresh shiitake mushrooms, stalks discarded, sliced
275g/10oz young spinach leaves, wilted
45ml/3 tbsp crème fraîche
salt and ground black pepper

1 Preheat the oven to 190°C/375°F/Gas 5. Line a 30 × 20cm/ 12 × 8in Swiss roll tin (jelly roll pan) with baking parchment, making sure that the paper rises well above the sides of the tin. Grease lightly with butter.

2 Melt 50g/2oz/¼ cup of the butter in a large, heavy pan. Stir in the flour and cook over a low heat, stirring constantly with a wooden spoon, for 1 minute, then gradually whisk in the milk. Bring the mixture to the boil, whisking constantly, and continue cooking, until the mixture thickens to a smooth sauce.

3 Simmer for 2 minutes, then mix in the chèvre and half the Parmesan. Cool for 5 minutes, then beat in the egg yolks and plenty of salt and pepper.

4 Whisk the egg whites until they form soft peaks. Stir a spoonful of the egg whites into the chèvre mixture to lighten it, then gently fold in the remainder. Spoon the mixture into the prepared tin, spread evenly and gently with a metal spatula and smooth the surface, then bake for 15–17 minutes, until the top feels just firm.

5 Remove the roulade from the oven and cool for a few minutes, then invert it on to a sheet of baking parchment dusted with the remaining Parmesan. Carefully remove and discard the lining paper. Roll the roulade up with the baking parchment inside and leave to cool completely.

6 Make the filling. Melt the remaining butter in a heavy frying pan and set aside 30ml/2 tbsp. Add the mushrooms to the pan and cook over a low heat, stirring occasionally, for about 3 minutes. Stir in the spinach and heat through briefly. Drain well, then stir in the crème fraîche. Season to taste with salt and pepper, then set aside to cool.

7 Preheat the oven to 190°C/375°F/Gas 5. Carefully unroll the roulade and spread the filling over the surface. Roll it up again and place, join side down, in an ovenproof dish. Brush with the reserved melted butter and sprinkle with the remaining Parmesan. Bake for 15 minutes, or until risen and golden brown. Serve immediately.

PASTA, PIZZA & GRAINS

Pasta is every cook's favourite ingredient because it cooks so quickly and, as it combines so well with vegetables or creamy cheese sauces, it is immensely popular with vegetarians. This chapter features unusual, sophisticated and utterly superb pasta recipes that will surprise and delight your guests. Whether delicately flavoured spaghetti dishes, home-made ravioli or gourmet gnocchi, pasta proves that it can be truly special.

Mini pizzas topped with wild mushrooms or pimiento and pine nuts make fabulous appetizers, canapés to serve with pre-dinner drinks or party food, while the full-size pizzas are so smothered with colourful and succulent vegetables and richly flavoured cheeses that you will be spoilt for choice.

From bulgur wheat to pearl barley, the range of grains available today is immense, but rice remains the most popular – and the king of all rice dishes must be risotto. Deceptively simple, this Italian classic requires some loving care and attention while it cooks, but it isn't difficult and its unique, creamy texture makes the effort worthwhile. In Italy, risotto is served as a *primo*, a first course that is of equal size and importance as the second, and the sophisticated, richly flavoured recipes in this chapter are ideally suited to this treatment. However, they are so delicious – and filling – that you could also serve them as a main course. As well as risottos, there are dinner party dishes based on a variety of grains, offering a tempting contrast of colours, textures and flavours that are guaranteed to impress and delight.

Tagliarini with White Truffle

There is nothing quite like the fragrance and flavour of rare Italian white truffles.

Serves 4
350g/12oz fresh tagliarini
75g/3oz/6 tbsp butter, diced

60ml/4 tbsp freshly grated
  Parmesan cheese
freshly grated nutmeg
1 small white truffle, about
  25–40g/1–1½oz
salt and ground black pepper

1 Bring a large pan of lightly salted water to the boil and cook the pasta until it is *al dente*. Immediately, drain it well and tip it into a large, warmed bowl.

2 Add the diced butter, grated Parmesan and a little freshly grated nutmeg. Season with salt and pepper to taste. Toss well until all the strands are coated in melted butter.

3 Divide the pasta equally among four warmed, individual bowls and shave paper-thin slivers of the white truffle on top. Serve immediately.

Farfalle with Dolcelatte Cream

Sweet and simple, this sauce has a light nutty tang from the blue cheese.

Serves 4
350g/12oz/3 cups dried farfalle
175g/6oz dolcelatte cheese, diced

150ml/¼ pint/⅓ cup double
  (heavy) cream
10ml/2 tsp chopped fresh sage
salt and ground black pepper
fresh sage leaves, to garnish

1 Bring a large pan of lightly salted water to the boil and cook the pasta until it is *al dente*.
2 Meanwhile, melt the cheese with the double cream in a pan, stirring frequently.
3 Drain the pasta and return to the pan. Pour in the sauce with the chopped sage and toss to coat. Serve garnished with sage.

Sardinian Ravioli

With their unusual mashed potato and mint filling, these ravioli are certainly special.

Serves 4–6
1 quantity Pasta Dough
plain (all-purpose) flour,
  for dusting
50g/2oz/¼ cup butter
50g/2oz/⅔ cup freshly grated
  Pecorino cheese

For the filling
400g/14oz potatoes, diced
65g/2½oz/generous ⅔ cup
  grated mature (sharp)
  Pecorino cheese
75g/3oz soft fresh
  Pecorino cheese
1 egg yolk
bunch of fresh mint, chopped
good pinch of saffron powder
salt and ground black pepper

1 Make the filling. Bring a pan of lightly salted water to the boil and cook the potatoes for 15–20 minutes, or until soft. Drain, tip into a bowl, then mash until smooth. Cool, then stir in the cheeses, egg yolk, mint, saffron and salt and pepper to taste.

2 Using a pasta machine, roll out one-quarter of the pasta into a 90cm/36in strip. Cut the strip into two 45cm/18in lengths.

3 With a fluted 10cm/4in cutter, cut out 4–5 discs from one of the strips. Using a heaped teaspoon, put a mound of filling on one side of each disc. Brush a little water around the edge of each disc, then fold the plain side of the disc over the filling to make a half-moon shape. Pleat the curved edge to seal.

4 Put the ravioli on floured dishtowels, sprinkle with flour and leave to dry. Repeat the process with the remaining dough to make 32–40 ravioli altogether.

5 Preheat the oven to 190°C/375°F/Gas 5. Bring a large pan of lightly salted water to the boil and cook the ravioli for 4–5 minutes. Meanwhile, melt the butter in a small pan.

6 Drain the ravioli, transfer to a large ovenproof dish and pour the melted butter over. Sprinkle with the grated Pecorino and bake in the oven for 10–15 minutes, until golden and bubbly. Leave to stand for 5 minutes before serving.

Pumpkin Gnocchi with Chanterelle Cream

Very much a gourmet dish, this is perfect for occasions when you want to impress.

Serves 4
450g/1lb peeled
  pumpkin, chopped
450g/1lb potatoes, unpeeled
2 egg yolks
200g/7oz/1¾ cups plain (all-
  purpose) flour, plus extra
  for dredging
pinch of ground allspice
1.5ml/¼ tsp ground cinnamon
pinch of freshly grated nutmeg

finely grated rind of ½ orange
50g/2oz/⅔ cup freshly shaved
  Parmesan cheese
salt and ground black pepper

For the sauce
30ml/2 tbsp olive oil
1 shallot, chopped
175g/6oz/2 cups fresh
  chanterelles, sliced
150ml/¼ pint/⅔ cup
  crème fraîche
a little milk or water
75ml/5 tbsp chopped
  fresh parsley

1 Preheat the oven to 180°C/350°F/Gas 4. Wrap the pumpkin in foil and bake for 30 minutes. Meanwhile, put the potatoes in a pan of cold water, add salt and bring to the boil. Cook for about 20 minutes, until tender. Drain, peel and set aside.

2 Add the pumpkin to the potato and pass through a potato ricer. Alternatively, press through a sieve. Mix in the egg yolks, flour, spices, orange rind and seasoning to make a soft dough.

3 Bring a pan of lightly salted water to the boil. Dredge a work surface with flour. Spoon the dough into a piping (pastry) bag with a 1cm/½in plain nozzle. Pipe a 15cm/6in sausage on the surface. Roll in flour and cut into 2.5cm/1in pieces. Mark lightly with a fork and cook for 3–4 minutes in the boiling water.

4 Make the sauce. Heat the oil in a pan and cook the shallot until soft. Add the chanterelles and cook briefly, then stir in the crème fraîche. Simmer and add milk or water, if required. Add the parsley and season. Transfer the gnocchi to bowls. Spoon all the sauce over the top. Sprinkle with Parmesan and serve.

Radicchio Pizza

A scone dough base and an interesting radicchio, leek and tomato topping make this a quick and easy dish.

Serves 2
25ml/5 tsp olive oil, plus
  extra for greasing and dipping
½ x 400g/14oz can
  chopped tomatoes
2 garlic cloves, crushed
pinch of dried basil
2 leeks, sliced
90g/3½ oz radicchio,
  coarsely chopped

20g/¾oz/¼ cup freshly grated
  Parmesan cheese
115g/4oz mozzarella
  cheese, sliced
10–12 pitted black olives
salt and ground black pepper
fresh basil leaves, to garnish

For the dough
225g/8oz/2 cups self-raising
  (self-rising) flour, plus extra
  for dusting
2.5ml/½ tsp salt
50g/2oz/¼ cup butter
about 120ml/4fl oz/½ cup milk

1 Preheat the oven to 220°C/425°F/Gas 7. Grease a baking sheet. Make the dough by mixing the flour and salt in a bowl, rubbing in the butter and gradually stirring in the milk. Roll the dough out on a lightly floured surface to a 25–28cm/10–11in round. Place this on the baking sheet.

2 Tip the tomatoes into a small pan. Stir in half the crushed garlic, together with the dried basil and a little seasoning. Simmer over a medium heat until the mixture is thick and has reduced by about half.

3 Heat the olive oil in a large frying pan and cook the leeks and remaining garlic until slightly softened. Add the radicchio and cook, stirring constantly, for 2–3 minutes, then cover and simmer gently for 5–10 minutes. Stir in the Parmesan cheese and season to taste with salt and pepper.

4 Cover the dough base with the tomato mixture, then spoon the leek and radicchio mixture on top. Arrange the mozzarella slices over the vegetables and sprinkle over the olives. Dip a few basil leaves in olive oil and arrange them on top. Bake for 15–20 minutes, until the base and top are golden brown.

Spring Vegetable & Pine Nut Pizza

Here's a chance to practise your artistic skills. With its colourful topping of tender young vegetables, the pizza looks like an artist's palette and it tastes wonderful.

Serves 2–3
25–30cm/10–12in pizza base
45ml/3 tbsp olive oil
1 garlic clove, crushed
4 spring onions (scallions), sliced
2 courgettes (zucchini), thinly sliced
1 leek, thinly sliced
115g/4oz asparagus tips, sliced
15ml/1 tbsp chopped fresh oregano
30ml/2 tbsp pine nuts
50g/2oz/1/2 cup grated mozzarella, cheese
30ml/2 tbsp freshly grated Parmesan cheese
salt and ground black pepper

For the tomato sauce
15ml/1 tbsp olive oil
1 onion, finely chopped
1 garlic clove, crushed
400ml/14oz can chopped tomatoes
15ml/1 tbsp tomato purée (paste)
15ml/1 tbsp chopped fresh herbs
pinch of sugar

1 Make the tomato sauce. Heat the oil in a pan and cook the onion and garlic over a low heat, stirring occasionally, for about 5 minutes, until softened. Add the remaining ingredients, stir well and simmer for 15–20 minutes, until the mixture is thick.

2 Preheat the oven to 220°C/425°F/Gas 7. Brush the pizza base with 15ml/1 tbsp of the olive oil, then spread the tomato sauce evenly over the top to within 1cm/½in of the edge.

3 Heat half the remaining olive oil in a frying pan and stir-fry the garlic, spring onions, courgettes, leek and asparagus over a medium heat for 3–5 minutes.

4 Arrange the vegetables over the tomato sauce, then sprinkle the oregano and pine nuts over the top.

5 Mix the cheeses and sprinkle over. Drizzle with the remaining olive oil and season well. Bake for 15–20 minutes, until crisp and golden. Serve immediately.

Roasted Vegetable & Goat's Cheese Pizza

This pizza incorporates the smoky flavours of roasted vegetables and the unique taste of goat's cheese.

Serves 3
1 aubergine (eggplant), cut into thick chunks
2 courgettes (zucchini), sliced lengthways
1 red (bell) pepper, quartered and seeded
1 yellow (bell) pepper, quartered and seeded
1 small red onion, cut into wedges
90ml/6 tbsp olive oil
25–30cm/10–12in pizza base
400g/14oz can chopped tomatoes, well drained
115g/4oz goat's cheese, cubed
15ml/1 tbsp chopped fresh thyme
ground black pepper
green olive tapenade (see Cook's Tip), to serve

1 Preheat the oven to 220°C/425°F/Gas 7. Place the vegetables in a roasting pan. Brush with 60ml/4 tbsp of the oil. Roast for 30 minutes, until charred, turning the peppers once. Remove the vegetables but leave the oven on.

2 Put the peppers in a bowl and cover with crumpled kitchen paper. When cool enough to handle, peel off the skins and cut the flesh into thick strips. Brush the pizza base with half the remaining oil and spread over the drained tomatoes. Arrange the roasted vegetables on top of the pizza. Dot with the goat's cheese and sprinkle over the thyme.

3 Drizzle over the remaining oil and season. Bake for 15–20 minutes, until crisp. Spoon the tapenade over to serve.

> **Cook's Tip**
> For vegetarian green olive tapenade, put 40 pitted green olives and 5ml/1 tsp capers in a food processor. Add four pieces of drained sun-dried tomatoes in oil, 5ml/1 tsp ground almonds, one chopped garlic clove and a pinch of ground cumin. Process briefly, add 60ml/4 tbsp olive oil and process to a paste.

Wild Mushroom Pizzettes

Serve these extravagant pizzas as an appetizer for special guests, or make miniature versions for serving with glasses of champagne or cocktails.

Serves 4
45ml/3 tbsp olive oil
350g/12oz/4½ cups fresh wild mushrooms, sliced
2 shallots, chopped
2 garlic cloves, finely chopped
30ml/2 tbsp chopped fresh mixed thyme and flat leaf parsley
1 quantity Pizza Dough
40g/1½oz/scant ½ cup grated Gruyère cheese
30ml/2 tbsp freshly grated Parmesan cheese
salt and ground black pepper

1 Preheat the oven to 220°C/425°F/Gas 7. Heat 30ml/2 tbsp of the oil in a frying pan. Add the mushrooms, shallots and garlic and cook over a medium heat, stirring occasionally, until all the juices have evaporated.

2 Stir in half the mixed herbs and season to taste with salt and pepper, then set aside to cool.

3 Divide the dough into four pieces and roll out each one on a lightly floured surface to a 13cm/5in round. Place well apart on two greased baking sheets, then push up the dough edges on each to form a thin rim. Brush the pizza bases with the remaining oil and top with the wild mushroom mixture, leaving a small rim all the way around.

4 Mix the Gruyère and Parmesan cheeses, then sprinkle one-quarter of the mixture over each of the pizzettes. Bake for 15–20 minutes, until crisp and golden. Remove from the oven and sprinkle over the remaining herbs to serve.

Cook's Tip
Fresh wild mushrooms add a distinctive flavour to the topping, but a mixture of cultivated mushrooms, such as shiitake, oyster and chestnut mushrooms, would do just as well.

Feta, Pimiento & Pine Nut Pizzettes

Perk up a party with these tempting mini pizzas. They take only minutes to make, a short time to cook and will be eaten even quicker.

Makes 24
double quantity Pizza Dough
60ml/4 tbsp olive oil
30ml/2 tbsp Vegetarian Green Olive Tapenade
175g/6oz feta cheese
1 large canned or bottled pimiento, drained
30ml/2 tbsp chopped fresh thyme
30ml/2 tbsp pine nuts
ground black pepper
fresh thyme sprigs, to garnish

1 Preheat the oven to 220°C/425°F/Gas 7. Divide the pizza dough into 24 pieces and roll out each one on a lightly floured surface to a small oval, about 3mm/⅛in thick.

2 Place well apart on greased baking sheets and prick all over with a fork. Brush with 30ml/2 tbsp of the oil.

3 Spread a thin layer of the tapenade on each oval and crumble over the feta. Cut the pimiento into thin strips and pile on top of the cheese.

4 Sprinkle each pizzette with thyme and pine nuts. Drizzle over the remaining oil and grind over plenty of black pepper. Bake for 10–15 minutes, until crisp and golden. Garnish with thyme sprigs and serve immediately.

Cook's Tip
Try to find ewe's milk feta, which has the best flavour.

Variations
• *Substitute goat's cheese for the feta.*
• *The tapenade can be made with pitted black, rather than green olives, if you like.*

Spinach & Ricotta Panzerotti

These make great party nibbles for serving with drinks or as appetizers.

Makes 20–24
115g/4oz frozen chopped
　spinach, thawed, drained and
　squeezed dry
50g/2oz/ ¼ cup ricotta cheese
50g/2oz/ ⅔ cup freshly grated
　Parmesan cheese

good pinch of freshly
　grated nutmeg
double quantity Pizza Dough
plain (all-purpose) flour,
　for dusting
1 egg white, lightly beaten
oil for deep-frying
salt and ground black pepper

1 Place the spinach, ricotta, Parmesan and nutmeg in a bowl. Season to taste with salt and pepper and beat until smooth.

2 Roll out the dough on a lightly floured surface to 3mm/ ⅛in thick. Stamp out 20–24 rounds with a 7.5cm/3in round cutter.

3 Spread a teaspoon of spinach mixture over one half of each round, then brush the edges of the dough with egg white, fold the dough over and press the edges firmly together to seal.

4 Heat the oil in a large heavy pan or deep-fat fryer to 180°C/350°F or until a cube of day-old bread, added to the oil, browns in 45–60 seconds. Deep-fry the panzerotti, a few at a time, for 2–3 minutes until golden. Drain on kitchen paper and serve immediately.

Cook's Tips
• Make sure the spinach is squeezed as dry as possible.
• It is important to make sure that oil for deep-frying is heated to the right temperature before adding the panzerotti.
• Do not crowd the pan, as this not only drastically lowers the temperature of the oil, but can also cause it to splash.
• Do serve these as soon as possible after frying, as they taste nowhere near so good if left to cool.

Aubergine & Sun-dried Tomato Calzone

Aubergines, shallots and sun-dried tomatoes make an unusual filling for calzone – pizza "turnovers".

Serves 2
45ml/3 tbsp olive oil
3 shallots, chopped
4 baby aubergines (eggplant), cut
　into small cubes
1 garlic clove, chopped
6 pieces of sun-dried tomatoes in
　oil, drained and chopped

1.5ml/ ¼ tsp dried red
　chilli flakes
10ml/2 tsp chopped fresh thyme
1 quantity Pizza Dough
plain (all-purpose) flour,
　for dusting
75g/3oz mozzarella, cubed
salt and ground black pepper
15–30ml/1–2 tbsp freshly grated
　Parmesan cheese, to serve

1 Preheat the oven to 220°C/425°F/Gas 7. Heat 30ml/2 tbsp of the oil in a heavy frying pan. Add the shallots and cook over a low heat, stirring occasionally, for 5 minutes, until softened.

2 Add the aubergines, garlic, sun-dried tomatoes, chilli flakes and thyme and season with salt and pepper to taste. Cook for 4–5 minutes, stirring frequently, until the aubergines are beginning to soften.

3 Divide the dough in half and roll out each piece on a lightly floured surface to an 18cm/7in round. Spread the aubergine mixture over half of each round, leaving a 2.5cm/1in border, then sprinkle over the mozzarella. Dampen the edges with water, then fold the dough over to enclose the filling. Press the edges firmly together to seal. Place the calzones on two greased baking sheets.

4 Brush with half the remaining oil and make a small hole in the top of each to let the steam escape. Bake the calzone for 15–20 minutes, until golden. Remove from the oven and brush with the remaining olive oil. Sprinkle over the grated Parmesan and serve immediately.

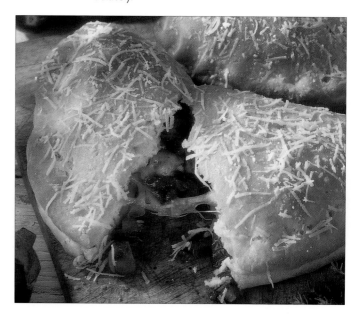

Bulgur Wheat, Asparagus and Broad Bean Pilaff

Nutty-textured bulgur wheat is usually simply soaked in boiling water until it is softened, but it can be cooked like rice to make a pilaff. Here it is combined with broad beans, herbs and lemon and orange rinds, which add a fresh, springtime flavour.

Serves 4
250g/9oz/1½ cups bulgur wheat
750–900ml/1¼–1½ pints/
   3–3¾ cups warm
   vegetable stock

225g/8oz asparagus spears
225g/8oz/2 cups frozen broad
   (fava) beans, thawed
8 spring onions (scallions),
   chopped
15ml/1 tbsp grated lemon rind
15ml/1 tbsp grated orange rind
40g/1½oz/3 tbsp butter, cut into
   small pieces
60ml/4 tbsp chopped fresh flat
   leaf parsley
30ml/2 tbsp chopped fresh dill,
   plus extra sprigs to garnish
salt and ground black pepper

1 If using a clay pot, soak in cold water for 20 minutes, then drain. Place the bulgur wheat in the clay pot or in a shallow, ovenproof earthenware dish and pour over 600ml/1 pint/2½ cups of the stock. Season with salt and pepper.

2 Cut the asparagus spears into 2.5cm/1in lengths, discarding any hard, woody ends from the stems. Add the asparagus pieces to the clay pot or dish and gently stir these into the bulgur wheat.

3 Cover the clay pot or dish tightly and place in an unheated oven. Set the oven to 200°C/400°F/Gas 6 and then cook the bulgur wheat and asparagus for 20 minutes.

4 Meanwhile, pop the broad beans out of their skins, and then stir the beans into the bulgur pilaff after it has cooked for about 20 minutes, adding a little more stock at the same time. Re-cover the clay pot or dish and return the dish to the oven for about 10 minutes.

5 Stir in the spring onions and grated lemon and orange rind. Add a little more stock, if necessary. Cover and return to the oven for 5 minutes.

6 Dot the pieces of butter over the top of the pilaff and leave to stand, covered, for 5 minutes.

7 Add the chopped parsley and dill to the pilaff and stir well with a fork to fluff up the bulgur wheat and distribute the herbs evenly. Check the seasoning and add salt and plenty of black pepper. Serve the pilaff hot, garnished with sprigs of fresh dill.

> **Cook's Tip**
> If your clay pot or earthenware dish doesn't have its own lid, then cover the pot or dish with foil, crimping it around the edge to seal. Or, if the top of the dish is completely flat, then you can simply place a flat, heavy baking sheet on top.

Grilled Polenta with Caramelized Onions

Slices of grilled polenta topped with caramelized onions and bubbling Taleggio cheese are extremely tasty.

Serves 4
900ml/1½ pints/3¾ cups water
5ml/1 tsp salt
150g/5oz/generous 1 cup polenta
   or cornmeal
50g/2oz/⅔ cup freshly grated
   Parmesan cheese

5ml/1 tsp chopped fresh thyme
90ml/6 tbsp olive oil
675g/1½ lb onions, halved
   and sliced
2 garlic cloves, chopped
a few fresh thyme sprigs
5ml/1 tsp soft light brown sugar
30ml/2 tbsp balsamic vinegar
2 heads radicchio, cut into thick
   slices or wedges
225g/7oz Taleggio cheese, sliced
salt and ground black pepper

1 Pour the water into a large pan, add the salt and bring to the boil. Adjust to a simmer. Stirring constantly, add the polenta in a steady stream, then bring to the boil. Immediately, reduce the heat to the lowest setting and cook, stirring frequently, for 30–40 minutes, until thick and smooth.

2 Beat in the Parmesan and chopped thyme, then tip the mixture on to a large tray. Spread evenly, then leave to set.

3 Heat 30ml/2 tbsp of the oil in a frying pan and cook the onions over a very low heat for 15 minutes, stirring occasionally. Add the garlic and some thyme sprigs. Cook for 10 minutes more, until golden and very soft. Add the sugar and half the vinegar. Season to taste. Cook for 10 minutes, until browned.

4 Preheat the grill (broiler). Thickly slice the polenta and brush with a little oil, then grill (broil) until lightly browned. Turn over. Add the radicchio to the grill rack, season and brush with a little oil. Grill for 5 minutes, until the polenta and radicchio are browned. Drizzle a little vinegar over the radicchio.

5 Heap the onions on the polenta. Sprinkle with the cheese and thyme sprigs. Grill until the cheese is bubbling, then serve.

Risotto with Four Cheeses

This is a very rich dish. Serve it as an appetizer for a special dinner party – preferably with a light, dry, sparkling white wine.

Serves 4
40g/1½oz/3 tbsp butter
1 small onion, finely chopped
1.2 litres/2 pints/5 cups well-flavoured vegetable stock
350g/12oz/1¾ cups risotto rice
200ml/7fl oz/scant 1 cup dry white wine
50g/2oz/½ cup grated Gruyère cheese
50g/2oz/½ cup diced Taleggio cheese
50g/2oz/½ cup diced Gorgonzola cheese
50g/2oz/⅔ cup freshly grated Parmesan cheese
salt and ground black pepper
chopped fresh flat leaf parsley, to garnish

1 Melt the butter in a large, heavy pan. Add the onion and cook over a low heat, stirring occasionally, for about 8 minutes, until softened and lightly browned. Pour the stock into another pan and heat it to simmering point. Lower the heat so that the stock is barely simmering.

2 Add the rice to the onion mixture, stir until all the grains start to swell and burst, then stir in the white wine. When most of it has been absorbed, pour in a little of the hot stock. Season with salt and pepper to taste. Stir over a low heat until the stock has been absorbed.

3 Gradually add the remaining stock, a little at a time, allowing the rice to absorb the liquid before adding more, and stirring constantly. After 20–25 minutes the rice will be *al dente* and the risotto creamy.

4 Turn off the heat under the pan, then add the Gruyère, Taleggio, Gorgonzola and half the Parmesan cheese. Stir gently until the cheeses have melted, then taste and adjust the seasoning, if necessary. Spoon the risotto into a warmed serving bowl and garnish with parsley. Serve immediately and hand the remaining Parmesan separately.

Risotto with Asparagus

Fresh farm asparagus is only in season for a short time. Make the most of it by inviting friends to share this elegant risotto.

Serves 3–4
225g/8oz fresh asparagus
750ml/1¼ pints/3 cups well-flavoured vegetable stock
65g/2½ oz/5 tbsp butter
1 small onion, finely chopped
275g/10oz/1½ cups risotto rice
75g/3oz/1 cup freshly grated Parmesan cheese
salt and ground black pepper

1 Snap the asparagus stalks and discard the woody ends. Bring a pan of water to the boil, add the asparagus and cook for 5 minutes. Drain, reserving the cooking water, refresh under cold water and drain well again. Cut the asparagus stalks diagonally into 4cm/1½in pieces. Keep the tips separate from the rest of the stalks.

2 Pour the stock into a pan and add 450ml/ ¾ pint/scant 2 cups of the reserved asparagus cooking water. Heat to simmering point.

3 Melt two-thirds of the butter in a large, heavy pan and cook the onion until soft and golden. Stir in all the asparagus except the tips. Cook for 2–3 minutes. Add the rice and cook for 1–2 minutes, stirring to coat the grains with butter. Add a ladleful of the hot stock and stir until it has been absorbed.

4 Gradually add the remaining hot stock, a little at a time, allowing the rice to absorb each addition before adding more and stirring constantly.

5 After 15 minutes of adding stock, mix in the asparagus tips. Continue to cook as before, for 5–10 minutes, until the rice is *al dente* and the risotto is creamy.

6 Remove from the heat, stir in the remaining butter and the Parmesan. Adjust the seasoning, if necessary. Serve immediately.

Porcini & Parmesan Risotto

The success of a good risotto depends on both the quality of the rice used and the technique. Add the stock gradually and stir constantly to create a creamy texture.

Serves 4

15g/½oz/¼ cup dried
   porcini mushrooms
150ml/ ¼ pint/ ⅔ cup
   warm water
1 litre/1¾ pints/4 cups well-
   flavoured vegetable stock
generous pinch of saffron threads
30ml/2 tbsp olive oil
1 onion, finely chopped
1 garlic clove, crushed
350g/12oz/1¾ cups risotto rice
150ml/ ¼ pint/ ⅔ cup dry
   white wine
25g/1oz/2 tbsp butter
50g/2oz/⅔ cup freshly grated
   Parmesan cheese
salt and ground black pepper
pink and yellow oyster
   mushrooms, to serve (optional)

1 Put the dried porcini in a bowl and pour over the warm water. Leave to soak for 20 minutes, then lift out the mushrooms with a slotted spoon. Filter the soaking water through a sieve lined with kitchen paper, then place it in a pan with the stock. Bring the liquid to a gentle simmer.

2 Spoon about 45ml/3 tbsp of the hot stock into a cup and stir in the saffron threads. Set aside. Finely chop the porcini. Heat the oil in a separate pan and lightly cook the onion, garlic and mushrooms for 5 minutes. Add the rice and stir to coat the grains in oil. Cook for 2 minutes, stirring constantly. Season with salt and pepper.

3 Pour in the white wine. Cook, stirring until it has been absorbed, then ladle in one-quarter of the stock. Cook, stirring constantly, until that has been absorbed, then gradually add the remaining stock, a little at a time. Allow the rice to absorb each batch of liquid before adding more and stir constantly.

4 After about 20 minutes, when all the stock has been absorbed and the rice is *al dente*, stir in the butter, saffron water (with the threads) and half the Parmesan. Serve, sprinkled with the remaining Parmesan and with oyster mushrooms, if you like.

Champagne Risotto

This may seem rather extravagant, but it makes a beautifully flavoured risotto, perfect for that special celebratory dinner.

Serves 3–4

25g/1oz/2 tbsp butter
2 shallots, finely chopped
275g/10oz/1½ cups risotto rice
½ bottle or 300ml/ ½ pint/
   1¼ cups champagne
750ml/1¼ pints/3 cups
   simmering light vegetable stock
150ml/ ¼ pint/ ⅔ cup double
   (heavy) cream
40g/1½ oz/ ½ cup freshly grated
   Parmesan cheese
10ml/2 tsp very finely chopped
   fresh chervil
salt and ground black pepper
black truffle shavings, to
   garnish (optional)

1 Melt the butter in a large, heavy pan. Add the shallots and cook over a low heat, stirring occasionally, for 2–3 minutes, until softened. Add the rice and cook, stirring constantly, until the grains are coated in butter.

2 Carefully pour in about two-thirds of the champagne so that it doesn't bubble over, and cook over a high heat, stirring constantly, until all the liquid has been absorbed.

3 Add the stock, a ladleful at a time, stirring constantly and making sure that each addition has been completely absorbed before adding more. The risotto should gradually become creamy and velvety and all the stock should be absorbed.

4 When the rice is tender, but retains a bit of "bite", stir in the remaining champagne with the double cream and Parmesan. Adjust the seasoning. Remove from the heat, cover and leave to stand for a few minutes. Stir in the chervil. If you want to enhance the flavour, garnish with a few truffle shavings.

Cook's Tip
When cooking a risotto of this calibre, it is especially important to use the correct type of rice. Carnaroli would be perfect.

Barley Risotto with Roasted Squash & Leeks

This is more like a nutty pilaff than a classic risotto. Sweet leeks and roasted squash are superb with pearl barley.

Serves 4–5
200g/7oz/scant 1 cup
   pearl barley
1 butternut squash, peeled,
   seeded and cut into chunks
10ml/2 tsp chopped fresh thyme
60ml/4 tbsp olive oil
25g/1oz/2 tbsp butter
4 leeks, cut diagonally into fairly
   thick slices

2 garlic cloves, finely chopped
175g/6oz/2¼ cups chestnut
   mushrooms, sliced
2 carrots, coarsely grated
about 120ml/4fl oz/ ½ cup
   vegetable stock
30ml/2 tbsp chopped fresh
   flat leaf parsley
50g/2oz Pecorino cheese, grated
   or shaved
45ml/3 tbsp pumpkin
   seeds, toasted
salt and ground black pepper

1 Rinse and drain the barley. Bring a pan of water to simmering point, add the barley and half-cover. Cook for 35–45 minutes, or until tender. Drain. Preheat the oven to 200°C/400°F/Gas 6.

2 Place the squash in a roasting pan with half the thyme. Season with pepper and toss with half the oil. Roast, stirring once, for 30–35 minutes, until tender and beginning to brown.

3 Heat half the butter with the remaining oil in a large frying pan. Cook the leeks and garlic gently for 5 minutes. Add the mushrooms and remaining thyme, then cook until the liquid from the mushrooms evaporates and they begin to brown.

4 Stir in the carrots and cook for 2 minutes, then add the barley and most of the stock. Season and partially cover. Cook for 5 minutes. Pour in the remaining stock if necessary. Stir in the parsley, the remaining butter and half the Pecorino, then the squash, with salt and pepper to taste. Serve, sprinkled with pumpkin seeds and the remaining Pecorino.

Risotto-stuffed Aubergines with Spicy Tomato Sauce

Dramatic good looks, plenty of substance and an interesting flavour make aubergines an excellent choice when entertaining.

Serves 4
4 small aubergines (eggplant)
105ml/7 tbsp olive oil
1 small onion, chopped
175g/6oz/scant 1 cup risotto rice
750ml/1¼ pints/3 cups hot
   vegetable stock

15ml/1 tbsp white wine vinegar
25g/1oz/ ⅓ cup freshly grated
   Parmesan cheese
30ml/2 tbsp pine nuts

For the tomato sauce
300ml/ ½ pint/1¼ cups thick
   passata (bottled strained
   tomatoes) or puréed tomatoes
5ml/1 tsp mild curry paste
pinch of salt

1 Preheat the oven to 200°C/400°F/Gas 6. Cut the aubergines in half lengthways, cross-hatch the flesh, then remove it with a small knife. Brush the shells with 30ml/2 tbsp of the oil and place on a baking sheet, supported by crumpled foil. Bake for 6–8 minutes. Set aside.

2 Chop the aubergine flesh. Heat the remaining oil in a large, heavy pan. Add the aubergine flesh and the onion and cook over a low heat, stirring occasionally, for 3–4 minutes, until softened but not coloured.

3 Stir in the rice and stock and simmer, uncovered, for about 15 minutes. Add the vinegar.

4 Increase the oven temperature to 230°C/450°F/Gas 8. Spoon the rice mixture into the aubergine skins, top with the cheese and pine nuts, return to the oven and brown for 5 minutes.

5 Meanwhile, make the sauce. Mix the passata or puréed tomatoes with the curry paste in a small pan. Heat through and add salt to taste. Spoon the sauce on to four individual serving plates and arrange two aubergine halves on each one.

Courgette Roulade

This makes an impressive buffet supper or dinner party dish.

Serves 6
40g/1½oz/3 tbsp butter
50g/2oz/½ cup plain (all-purpose) flour
300ml/½ pint/1¼ cups milk
4 eggs, separated
3 courgettes (zucchini), grated
25g/1oz/⅓ cup freshly grated Parmesan cheese, plus 30ml/ 2 tbsp for sprinkling
salt and ground black pepper

herb and green leaf salad, to serve

For the filling
75g/3oz/scant ½ cup soft goat's cheese
60ml/4 tbsp fromage frais or ricotta
225g/8oz/2 cups cooked rice
15ml/1 tbsp chopped mixed fresh herbs
15ml/1 tbsp olive oil
15g/½oz/1 tbsp butter
75g/3oz/1¼ cups button (white) mushrooms, finely chopped

1 Preheat the oven to 200°C/400°F/Gas 6. Line a 33 × 23cm/ 13 × 9in Swiss roll tin (jelly roll pan) with baking parchment.

2 Melt the butter in a pan, stir in the flour and cook, stirring, for 1–2 minutes. Gradually stir in the milk until the mixture forms a smooth sauce. Remove from the heat and cool. Stir in the egg yolks, add the courgettes and the Parmesan and season.

3 Whisk the egg whites until stiff, fold them into the courgette mixture and scrape into the prepared tin. Spread evenly. Bake for 10–15 minutes, until firm and lightly golden. Carefully turn out on to a sheet of baking parchment sprinkled with 30ml/ 2 tbsp grated Parmesan. Peel away the lining paper. Roll the roulade up, using the paper as a guide, and leave it to cool.

4 To make the filling, mix the goat's cheese, fromage frais, rice and herbs in a bowl. Season with salt and pepper. Heat the oil and butter in a pan and cook the mushrooms until soft.

5 Unwrap the roulade, spread with the rice filling and lay the mushrooms along the centre. Roll up again. Serve with a herb and green leaf salad.

Wild Rice with Grilled Vegetables

The mixture of wild rice and long grain rice in this dish works very well, and makes an extremely tasty vegetarian meal.

Serves 4
225g/8oz/generous 1 cup mixed wild and long grain rice
1 large aubergine (eggplant), thickly sliced
1 red (bell) pepper, seeded and cut into quarters
1 yellow (bell) pepper, seeded and cut into quarters
1 green (bell) pepper, seeded and cut into quarters

2 red onions, sliced
225g/8oz/3 cups brown cap (cremini) or shiitake mushrooms
2 small courgettes (zucchini), cut in half lengthways
olive oil, for brushing
30ml/2 tbsp chopped fresh thyme, plus whole sprigs to garnish (optional)

For the dressing
90ml/6 tbsp extra virgin olive oil
30ml/2 tbsp balsamic vinegar
2 garlic cloves, crushed
salt and ground black pepper

1 Put the wild and long grain rice in a large pan of cold salted water. Bring to the boil, then lower the heat, cover and cook gently for 30–40 minutes (or according to the instructions on the packet), until tender.

2 Preheat the grill (broiler). Make the dressing by whisking the olive oil with the vinegar and garlic in a bowl, then season.

3 Arrange all the vegetables on a grill rack. Brush with olive oil and grill (broil) for about 5 minutes.

4 Turn the vegetables over, brush them with more olive oil and grill for 5–8 minutes more, or until tender and beginning to char in places.

5 Drain the rice, tip into a bowl and toss in half the dressing. Spoon on to individual plates and arrange the grilled vegetables on top. Pour over the remaining dressing, sprinkle over the chopped thyme and serve. Whole thyme sprigs can be used as a garnish, if you like.

STUFFED VEGETABLES, BAKED DISHES, CRÊPES & PASTRY DISHES

This chapter offers a superb collection of dishes that really demonstrates the versatility of vegetarian cooking. Stuffed vegetables and filled crêpes are perennial favourites, popular with both adults and children, but these recipes offer less usual combinations, providing a new twist to the theme. Vegetables such as kohlrabi and Jerusalem artichokes take centre stage in fabulous main course dishes that are as pleasing to the eye as they are to the palate.

Pastry, whether filo, puff or shortcrust, and a medley of vegetables make a magical combination with their superb contrast of crisp, light-as-air crust and succulent filling or topping. Strudels, tarts, pies and flans, filled with onions, leeks, asparagus, cheese, courgettes (zucchini), aubergines (eggplant) or (bell) peppers look marvellous, smell wonderfully appetizing and taste superb. There are recipes for the confident cook that include making the dough as well as the filling, but if you are less experienced or simply pushed for time, you can use ready-made pastry – the results will still look impressive and taste home-made. Flans, tarts and pies that are served cold are ideal for parties and look very elegant on a buffet table.

Gougères, made with choux pastry and a savoury filling, always look spectacular, yet they are among the easiest and quickest of dishes to prepare, making them the perfect choice for easy entertaining.

Like pies and tarts, baked dishes can be prepared in advance, so you can safely leave them in the oven to cook while you spend time with your guests. Then all you have to do is the final sauce and garnish before serving. Meanwhile, the delicious aroma as they cook will have the taste buds tingling before anyone even sits down at the table.

Kohlrabi Stuffed with Peppers

If you haven't sampled kohlrabi, or have eaten it only in stews where its flavour is lost, do try this delectable dish.

Serves 4

4 small kohlrabi, about 175g/ 6oz each
about 400ml/14fl oz/1⅔ cups hot vegetable stock

15ml/1 tbsp sunflower oil
1 onion, chopped
1 small red (bell) pepper, seeded and sliced
1 small green (bell) pepper, seeded and sliced
salt and ground black pepper

1 Preheat the oven to 180°C/350°F/Gas 4. Trim the kohlrabi, then arrange them in a single layer in the base of a large, ovenproof dish.

2 Pour over the hot stock to come about halfway up the kohlrabi. Cover and braise in the oven for about 30 minutes, until tender. Transfer to a plate, reserving the stock, and leave to cool. Leave the oven on.

3 Heat the sunflower oil in a large, heavy frying pan. Add the onion and cook over a low heat, stirring occasionally, for 3–4 minutes, until softened. Add the red and green pepper slices and cook, stirring occasionally, for 2–3 minutes more, until the onion is lightly browned.

4 Add the reserved vegetable stock and season to taste with salt and pepper, then simmer, uncovered, until most of the stock has evaporated.

5 Scoop out the flesh from the kohlrabi and chop it coarsely. Stir the kohlrabi flesh into the onion and pepper mixture, taste and adjust the seasoning, if necessary. Arrange the shells in a shallow ovenproof dish.

6 Spoon the filling into the kohlrabi shells. Place in the oven for about 10 minutes to heat through, then serve.

Cabbage Roulades with Lemon Sauce

Cabbage or Swiss chard leaves, filled with a rice and red lentil stuffing, and served with a light egg and lemon sauce make a light and tasty main course.

Serves 4–6

12 large cabbage or Swiss chard leaves, stalks removed
25ml/2 tbsp sunflower oil
1 onion, chopped
1 large carrot, grated
115g/4oz/1½ cups sliced mushrooms

600ml/1 pint/2½ cups vegetable stock
115g/4oz/generous ½ cup long grain rice
60ml/4 tbsp red lentils
5ml/1 tsp dried oregano
90g/3½ oz soft cheese with garlic
25g/1oz/¼ cup plain (all-purpose) flour
juice of 1 lemon
3 eggs, beaten
salt and ground black pepper

1 Bring a large pan of lightly salted water to the boil. Add the cabbage or chard leaves, in batches if necessary, and blanch briefly until they are just beginning to wilt. Drain thoroughly, reserving the cooking water. Pat the leaves dry with kitchen paper and set aside.

2 Heat the oil in a large pan. Add the onion, carrot and mushrooms and cook over a low heat, stirring occasionally, for 5 minutes, until the onion is softened but not coloured.

3 Pour the stock into the pan, then stir in the rice, lentils and oregano. Bring to the boil over a medium heat. Cover, lower the heat and simmer gently for 15 minutes. Remove the pan from the heat and stir in the cheese. Season to taste.

4 Preheat the oven to 190°C/375°F/Gas 5. Lay each leaf in turn on a board, rib side down, and spoon a little of the filling on to the stalk end. Fold in the sides and roll up.

5 Place the roulades in a small roasting pan, seam side down, and pour in the reserved cooking water. Cover with foil and bake for 30–45 minutes, until the leaves are tender. Lift out the roulades with a slotted spoon and place them on a warmed serving dish. Reserve the cooking liquid. Keep the roulades warm while you make the sauce.

6 Strain 600ml/1 pint/2½ cups of the cooking liquid into a pan and bring to the boil. Blend the flour to a paste with a little cold water and whisk into the boiling liquid, together with the lemon juice.

7 Beat the eggs with about 60ml/4 tbsp of the hot liquid in a heatproof jug (pitcher). Gradually pour the mixture back into the pan of thickened liquid, whisking constantly. Continue to whisk over a very low heat until smooth and thick. Do not allow the sauce to boil or it will curdle.

8 Serve the roulades with some of the sauce poured over and the rest handed separately.

Summer Herb Ricotta Flan

Made without pastry, this delicate flan, flavoured with aromatic herbs, is ideal for a light lunch.

Serves 4
olive oil, for greasing and glazing
800g/1¾lb/3½ cups
   ricotta cheese
75g/3oz/1 cup freshly grated
   Parmesan cheese
3 eggs, separated
60ml/4 tbsp torn fresh
   basil leaves
60ml/4 tbsp chopped fresh chives
45ml/3 tbsp fresh oregano leaves
2.5ml/½ tsp salt
2.5ml/½ tsp paprika
ground black pepper
fresh herb leaves, to garnish

**For the black olive
purée (paste)**
400g/14oz/3½ cups pitted black
   olives, rinsed and halved
5 garlic cloves, crushed
75ml/5 tbsp olive oil

1 Preheat the oven to 180°C/350°F/Gas 4. Lightly grease a 23cm/9in springform cake tin (pan) with oil. Mix the ricotta, Parmesan and egg yolks in a food processor. Add the fresh herbs, with the salt and a little pepper. Process until smooth and creamy, then scrape into a bowl.

2 Whisk the egg whites in a large bowl until they form soft peaks. Gently fold the egg whites into the ricotta mixture. Spoon the mixture into the prepared tin and smooth the surface with a metal spatula.

3 Bake for 1 hour 20 minutes, or until the flan has risen and the top is golden. Remove from the oven and brush lightly with olive oil, then sprinkle with paprika. Leave the flan to cool before removing it from the tin.

4 Make the olive purée. Set aside a few olives for garnishing, if you like. Place the remainder in a food processor, add the garlic and process until finely chopped. With the motor running, gradually add the olive oil through the feeder tube until the mixture forms a coarse paste. Transfer it to a serving bowl. Garnish the flan with the herb leaves. Serve with the black olive purée.

Wild Mushroom Brioche with Orange Butter Sauce

A butter-rich brioche, ribboned with a mushroom duxelles would make an impressive centrepiece for a sophisticated dinner party.

Serves 4
5ml/1 tsp easy-blend (rapid-rise)
   dried yeast
45ml/3 tbsp milk, at
   room temperature
400g/14oz/3½ cups strong white
   bread flour
5ml/1 tsp salt
15ml/1 tbsp caster
   (superfine) sugar
3 eggs
finely grated rind of ½ lemon
200g/7oz/scant 1 cup
   butter, diced

For the filling
50g/2oz/¼ cup butter
2 shallots, chopped
350g/12oz/4 cups assorted wild
   and cultivated mushrooms,
   coarsely chopped
½ garlic clove, crushed
75ml/5 tbsp chopped
   fresh parsley
salt and ground black pepper

For the sauce
30ml/2 tbsp frozen concentrated
   orange juice
175g/6oz/¾ cup butter, diced
cayenne pepper

1 Dissolve the yeast in the milk, add 115g/4oz/1 cup of the flour and mix to form a dough. Fill a large bowl with lukewarm water, then place the bowl of dough in the water. Set aside for 30 minutes.

2 Place the remaining flour in a food processor fitted with the dough blade. Add the salt, sugar, eggs, lemon rind and the risen dough and process briefly to mix. Add the butter, in small pieces, and process until the dough is silky smooth and very slack. Wrap it in clear film (plastic wrap) and chill for 2 hours.

3 Make the filling. Melt the butter in a large, heavy frying pan. Add the shallots and cook over a low heat, stirring occasionally, until softened but not browned. Add the mushrooms and garlic and cook, stirring occasionally, until the juices begin to run. Increase the heat to medium to reduce the moisture. When dry, tip the mixture into a bowl, add the parsley and season to taste with salt and pepper.

4 Grease and line a 900g/2lb loaf tin (pan). Roll out the dough to a 15 x 30cm/6 x 12in rectangle. Spoon the cooked mushroom mixture over the dough and roll up to make a fat sausage. Drop this into the loaf tin, cover with a damp dishtowel and set aside in a warm place for 50 minutes, or until the dough has risen above the level of the rim.

5 Preheat the oven to 190°C/375°F/Gas 5, then bake the brioche for 40 minutes.

6 Meanwhile, make the sauce. Place the orange juice concentrate in a heatproof bowl set over a pan of simmering water. Remove from the heat and gradually whisk in the butter until creamy. Season to taste with cayenne, cover and keep warm. Turn out the brioche, slice and serve with the sauce.

Artichoke & Leek Crêpes

Fill thin crêpes with a mouthwatering soufflé mixture of Jerusalem artichokes and leek.

Serves 4
115g/4oz/1 cup plain (all-
  purpose) flour
pinch of salt
1 egg
300ml/ ½ pint/1 ¼ cups milk
vegetable oil, for greasing
fresh flat leaf parsley, to garnish

For the filling
50g/2oz/ ¼ cup butter
450g/1lb Jerusalem
  artichokes, diced
1 large leek, thinly sliced
30ml/2 tbsp self-raising (self-
  rising) flour
30ml/2 tbsp single (light) cream
75g/3oz/ ¾ cup grated mature
  (sharp) Cheddar cheese
30ml/2 tbsp chopped
  fresh parsley
freshly grated nutmeg
2 eggs, separated
salt and ground black pepper

1 Make the batter by blending the flour, salt, egg and milk to a smooth batter in a blender or food processor. Heat a lightly greased frying pan and add one-eighth of the batter. Cook for 2–3 minutes, then turn over and cook the other side for 2 minutes. Slide the crêpe out of the pan. Make seven more.

2 Make the filling. Melt the butter in a pan, add the artichokes and leek, cover and cook gently for about 12 minutes, until very soft. Mash with the back of a wooden spoon. Season well.

3 Stir the flour into the vegetables and cook for 1 minute. Take the pan off the heat and beat in the cream, cheese, parsley and nutmeg to taste. Cool, then add the egg yolks.

4 Preheat the oven to 190°C/375°F/Gas 5. Lightly grease a small ovenproof dish. Whisk the egg whites to soft peaks and carefully fold them into the leek and artichoke mixture.

5 Fold each crêpe in four, hold the top open and spoon the mixture into the centre. Arrange the crêpes in the dish, with the filling uppermost. Bake for 15 minutes, then serve immediately, garnished with parsley.

Roast Asparagus Crêpes

Roast asparagus is truly delicious – good enough to eat just as it is. However, for a really splendid dish, try this simple recipe.

Serves 3
175g/6oz/1 ½ cups plain (all-
  purpose) flour
2 eggs
350ml/12fl oz/1 ½ cups milk
vegetable oil, for frying

For the filling
90–120ml/6–8 tbsp olive oil
450g/1lb fresh asparagus
175g/6oz/ ¾ cup
  mascarpone cheese
60ml/4 tbsp single (light) cream
25g/1oz/ ⅓ cup freshly grated
  Parmesan cheese
sea salt

1 Make the crêpe batter by blending the flour, eggs, milk and a pinch of salt in a blender or food processor.

2 Heat a 20cm/8in frying pan, grease it lightly with vegetable oil and add one-sixth of the batter to make a crêpe. Cook for 2–3 minutes, then turn over and cook the other side until golden. Slide out of the pan and set aside. Cook five more crêpes in the same way.

3 Preheat the oven to 180°C/350°F/Gas 4. Lightly grease a large, shallow ovenproof dish. Arrange the asparagus in a single layer in the dish, drizzle over the remaining olive oil and gently shake the dish to coat each asparagus spear.

4 Sprinkle the asparagus with a little sea salt, then roast for 8–12 minutes, until tender.

5 Mix the mascarpone with the cream and Parmesan, beating well to combine, and spread a generous tablespoonful of the mixture over each crêpe, reserving little for the topping. Preheat the grill.

6 Divide the asparagus spears among the crêpes, roll up and arrange in a single layer in an ovenproof dish. Spoon over the remaining cheese mixture and grill for 4–5 minutes, then serve.

Party Purses

Filo "money bags" filled with creamy leeks make a very attractive dinner party dish.

Serves 4

115g/4oz/ ¹/₂ cup butter
225g/8oz leeks, trimmed and finely chopped
225g/8oz/1 cup cream cheese
15ml/1 tbsp finely chopped fresh dill
15ml/1 tbsp finely chopped fresh parsley
2 spring onions (scallions), finely chopped
pinch of cayenne pepper
1 garlic clove, finely chopped
1 egg yolk
9 sheets filo pastry, thawed if frozen
salt and ground black pepper
lightly cooked leeks, to serve

1 Preheat the oven to 200°C/400°F/Gas 6. Melt 25g/1oz/ 2 tbsp of the butter in a frying pan and cook the leeks for 4–5 minutes, until soft. Drain off any liquid.

2 Put the cream cheese in a bowl and stir in the dill, parsley, spring onions, cayenne and garlic. Stir in the egg yolk and leeks and season well. Melt the remaining butter.

3 Place one sheet of filo pastry on a board, brush with a little of the melted butter and place another sheet on top. Brush again with butter and top with a third sheet of filo.

4 Cut the layered filo into four squares and place 20ml/4 tsp of the cheese mixture in the centre of each square. Gather up the edges into a "bag", twisting the top to seal. Repeat with the remaining filo to make 12 bags. Brush them with a little butter.

5 Place the bags on a greased baking sheet and bake for 20–25 minutes, until golden brown. Serve on a bed of lightly cooked leeks.

> **Cook's Tip**
> *For an attractive effect, tie each bag with a strip of blanched leek before serving.*

Ratatouille & Fontina Strudel

Mix a colourful jumble of ratatouille vegetables with chunks of creamy cheese, wrap in filo and bake for a summery party pastry.

Serves 6

1 small aubergine (eggplant), diced
45ml/3 tbsp extra virgin olive oil
1 onion, sliced
2 garlic cloves, crushed
1 red (bell) pepper, seeded and sliced
1 yellow (bell) pepper, seeded and sliced
2 courgettes (zucchini), cut into small chunks
generous pinch of dried mixed herbs
30ml/2 tbsp pine nuts
30ml/2 tbsp raisins
8 filo pastry sheets, each about 30 x 18cm/12 x 7in, thawed if frozen
50g/2oz/¹/₄ cup butter, melted
130g/4¹/₂ oz Fontina or Bel Paese cheese, cut into small cubes
salt and ground black pepper
dressed mixed salad, to serve

1 Layer the aubergine in a colander, sprinkling each layer with salt. Drain for 20 minutes, then rinse, drain and pat dry.

2 Heat the oil in a large frying pan and gently cook the onion, garlic, peppers and aubergine for about 10 minutes. Add the courgettes and herbs and season with salt and pepper to taste. Cook for 5 minutes, until softened. Cool to room temperature, then stir in the pine nuts and raisins.

3 Preheat the oven to 180°C/350°F/Gas 4. Brush two sheets of filo pastry with a little melted butter. Lay the filo sheets side by side, overlapping them by 5cm/2in, to make a large rectangle.

4 Cover with the remaining filo, in the same way, brushing each layer with a little of the melted butter. Spoon the vegetable mixture down one long side of the filo.

5 Sprinkle the cheese over, then roll up to a long sausage. Transfer to a non-stick baking sheet and curl around to form a ring. Brush with the remaining melted butter and bake for 30 minutes, until golden. Cool for 10 minutes, then slice and serve with a mixed salad.

Asparagus Filo Wraps

For a taste sensation, try tender asparagus spears wrapped in crisp filo pastry. The buttery herb sauce makes the perfect partner.

Serves 2
4 sheets of filo pastry, thawed
    if frozen
50g/2oz/ ¼ cup butter, melted
16 young asparagus
    spears, trimmed
salad leaves, to garnish (optional)

For the sauce
2 shallots, finely chopped
1 bay leaf
150ml/ ¼ pint/ ⅔ cup dry
    white wine
175g/6oz/ ¾ cup butter, softened
15ml/1 tbsp chopped fresh herbs
salt and ground black pepper
chopped fresh chives, to garnish

1 Preheat the oven to 200°C/400°F/Gas 6. Keeping the rest of the filo covered with a damp dishtowel, brush each sheet with melted butter and fold one corner down to the bottom edge to create a wedge shape.

2 Lay four asparagus spears on top at the longest edge and roll up towards the shortest edge. Using the remaining filo and asparagus spears, make three more rolls in the same way.

3 Lay the rolls on a greased baking sheet. Brush with the remaining melted butter. Bake the rolls for 8 minutes, until the pastry is golden.

4 Meanwhile, make the sauce. Mix the shallots, bay leaf and wine in a pan. Cook over a high heat until the wine is reduced to about 45–60ml/3–4 tbsp.

5 Strain the wine mixture into a bowl. Whisk in the butter, a little at a time, until the sauce is smooth and glossy.

6 Stir in the herbs and add salt and pepper to taste. Return to the pan and warm through gently. Serve the rolls on individual plates with salad, if you like. Serve the butter sauce separately, sprinkled with a few chopped chives.

Asparagus & Ricotta Tart

The melt-in-the-mouth filling in this summery tart has a much more delicate texture than a quiche – and tastes absolutely wonderful.

Serves 4
175g/6oz/1 ½ cups plain (all-
    purpose) flour, plus extra
    for dusting
75g/3oz/6 tbsp butter

For the filling
225g/8oz asparagus
2 eggs, beaten
225g/8oz/1 cup ricotta cheese
30ml/2 tbsp Greek (US strained
    plain) yogurt
40g/1 ½oz/ ½ cup freshly grated
    Parmesan cheese
salt and ground black pepper

1 Preheat the oven to 200°C/400°F/Gas 6. Mix the flour and a pinch of salt in a bowl and rub in the butter with your fingertips or a pastry blender until the mixture resembles fine breadcrumbs. Stir in enough cold water to form a smooth dough and knead lightly on a floured surface.

2 Roll out the pastry on a lightly floured surface and then use to line a 23cm/9in flan ring (quiche pan). Prick the base all over with a fork. Bake the tart case (pie shell) for 10 minutes, until the pastry is pale but firm. Remove from the oven and reduce the temperature to 180°C/350°F/Gas 4.

3 Make the filling. Snap the asparagus and discard the woody ends. Cut off the tips and chop the remaining stalks into 2.5cm/1in pieces. Bring a pan of water to the boil. Blanch the stalks for 1 minute, then add the tips. Simmer for 4–5 minutes, until almost tender, then drain and refresh under cold water. Drain again. Separate the stalks from the asparagus tips.

4 Beat the eggs, ricotta, yogurt and Parmesan in a bowl. Stir in the asparagus stalks, season to taste with salt and pepper and pour the mixture into the pastry case.

5 Arrange the asparagus tips on top, pressing them down slightly into the ricotta mixture. Bake for 35–40 minutes, until golden. Serve warm or cold.

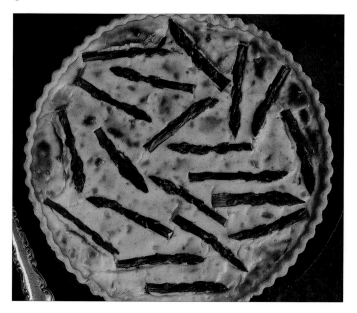

Potato & Leek Filo Pie

This makes an attractive centrepiece for a buffet.

Serves 8
800g/1¾lb new potatoes, thinly sliced
75g/3oz/6 tbsp butter
400g/14oz leeks, sliced
15g/½oz/½ cup parsley, finely chopped
60ml/4 tbsp chopped mixed fresh herbs
12 sheets filo pastry, thawed if frozen
150g/5oz white Cheshire, Lancashire or Cantal cheese, sliced
2 garlic cloves, finely chopped
250ml/8fl oz/1 cup double (heavy) cream
2 large (US extra large) egg yolks
salt and ground black pepper

1 Preheat the oven to 190°C/375°F/Gas 5. Bring a pan of lightly salted water to the boil and cook the potato slices for 3–4 minutes. Drain carefully.

2 Melt 25g/1oz/2 tbsp of the butter in a frying pan and cook the leeks gently, stirring occasionally, until softened. Remove from the heat, season with pepper and stir in half the parsley and half the mixed herbs.

3 Melt the remaining butter. Line a 23cm/9in round loose-based cake tin (pan) with six or seven sheets of filo, brushing each layer with butter. Let the edges of the pastry overhang the tin.

4 Layer the potatoes, leeks and cheese in the tin, sprinkling herbs and the garlic between the layers. Season. Flip the overhanging pastry over the filling and cover with two sheets of filo, tucking in the sides and brushing with melted butter. Cover the pie loosely with foil and bake for 35 minutes.

5 Meanwhile, beat the cream, egg yolks and remaining herbs together. Make a hole in the centre of the pie and gradually pour in the eggs and cream. Arrange the remaining pastry on top, teasing it into swirls, then brush with melted butter. Reduce the oven temperature to 180°C/350°F/Gas 4 and bake the pie for another 25–30 minutes. Leave to cool before serving.

Spanakopitta

This popular spinach and filo pastry pie comes from Greece. There are several ways of making it, but feta or Kefalotiri cheese is inevitably included.

Serves 6
1kg/2¼lb fresh spinach
4 spring onions (scallions), chopped
300g/11oz feta or Kefalotiri cheese, crumbled
2 large (US extra large) eggs, beaten
30ml/2 tbsp chopped fresh parsley
15ml/1 tbsp chopped fresh dill
about 8 filo pastry sheets, each about 30 x 18cm/12 x 7in, thawed if frozen
150ml/¼ pint/⅔ cup olive oil
ground black pepper

1 Preheat the oven to 190°C/375°F/Gas 5. Break off any thick stalks from the spinach, then wash the leaves and cook them in just the water that clings to the leaves in a heavy pan. As soon as they have wilted, drain them, refresh under cold water and drain again. Squeeze dry and chop coarsely.

2 Place the spinach in a bowl. Add the spring onions and cheese, then pour in the eggs. Mix in the herbs and season the filling with pepper.

3 Brush a filo sheet with oil and fit it into a 23cm/9in pie dish, allowing it to hang over the edge. Top with three or four more sheets; place these at different angles and brush each one with more oil, to make a coarsely shaped pie case.

4 Spoon in the filling, then top with all but one of the remaining filo sheets. Brush each filo sheet with oil. Fold in the over-hanging filo to seal in the filling. Brush the reserved filo with oil and scrunch it over the top of the pie.

5 Brush the pie with oil. Sprinkle with a little water to stop the filo edges from curling, then place on a baking sheet. Bake for about 40 minutes, until golden and crisp. Cool the pie for 15 minutes before serving.

Puff Pastry Boxes filled with Spring Vegetables in Pernod Sauce

Pernod gives the vegetables an extra special flavour.

Serves 4
225g/8oz puff pastry, thawed if frozen
15ml/1 tbsp freshly grated Parmesan cheese, plus extra
15ml/1 tbsp chopped fresh parsley
beaten egg, to glaze
175g/6oz/1 cup broad (fava) beans
115g/4oz baby carrots, scraped
8 spring onions (scallions), sliced
75g/3oz/³⁄₄ cup peas
50g/2oz/ ¹⁄₂ cup mangetouts (snow peas)
salt and ground black pepper
fresh dill sprigs, to garnish

For the sauce
200g/7oz can chopped tomatoes
25g/1oz/2 tbsp butter
25g/1oz/ ¹⁄₄ cup plain (all-purpose) flour
pinch of granulated sugar
45ml/3 tbsp chopped fresh dill
300ml/¹⁄₂ pint/1 ¹⁄₄ cups water
15ml/1 tbsp Pernod

1 Preheat the oven to 220°C/425°F/Gas 7. Grease a baking sheet. Roll out the pastry. Sprinkle with Parmesan and parsley, fold and roll out, then cut out four 7.5 x 10cm/3 x 4in rectangles. Lift them on to the baking sheet. Cut an inner oblong 1cm/ ¹⁄₂in from the edge on each, cutting halfway through. Score criss-cross lines on top of the inner rectangles, brush with egg and bake for 12–15 minutes, until golden.

2 Meanwhile, make the sauce. Press the tomatoes through a sieve into a pan, add the remaining ingredients and bring to the boil, stirring. Season, lower the heat and simmer until required.

3 Bring a pan of salted water to the boil. Cook the beans for 8 minutes. Add the carrots, onions and peas, cook for 5 minutes more, then add the mangetouts. Cook for 1 minute. Drain well.

4 Cut out the inner pieces from the pastry boxes. Swirl sauce on to four plates. Half-fill each box with vegetables, spoon over some sauce, then top up with vegetables. Sprinkle with cheese and place on the plates. Garnish with dill, add the lids and serve.

Courgette & Dill Tart

It is worth making your own pastry for this tart. Using a mixture of wholemeal flour and self-raising white flour gives very good results.

Serves 4
115g/4oz/1 cup plain wholemeal (whole-wheat) flour
115g/4oz/1 cup self-raising (self-rising) white flour
115g/4oz/¹⁄₂ cup chilled butter, diced
75ml/5 tbsp iced water
fresh dill sprigs, to garnish

For the filling
15ml/1 tbsp sunflower oil
3 courgettes (zucchini), sliced
2 egg yolks
150ml/ ¹⁄₄ pint/ ²⁄₃ cup double (heavy) cream
1 garlic clove, crushed
15ml/1 tbsp finely chopped fresh dill
salt and ground black pepper

1 Mix the flours in a food processor. Add a pinch of salt and the butter and pulse until the mixture resembles fine breadcrumbs. Gradually add the water until the mixture forms a dough. Wrap and chill for 30 minutes.

2 Preheat the oven to 200°C/400°F/Gas 6. Grease a 20cm/8in flan tin (quiche pan). Roll out the pastry and ease it into the tin. Prick the base and bake for 10–15 minutes until golden.

3 Meanwhile, make the filling. Heat the oil in a frying pan and cook the courgettes for 2–3 minutes, until lightly browned. Mix the egg yolks, cream, garlic and dill in a small bowl. Season to taste with salt and pepper.

4 Layer the courgette slices in circles in the pastry case (pie shell). Pour over the cream mixture. Bake for 25–30 minutes, or until the filling is firm and lightly golden. Cool in the tin, then transfer to a board or plate. Garnish with dill and serve.

Cook's Tip
If you don't have a food processor, rub the butter into the flour mixture by hand.

Leek & Roquefort Tart with Walnut Pastry

Mild leeks go exceptionally well with the salty flavour of Roquefort cheese.

Serves 4–6
25g/1oz/2 tbsp butter
450g/1lb leeks (trimmed weight), sliced
175g/6oz Roquefort cheese, sliced
2 large (US extra large) eggs
250ml/8fl oz/1 cup double (heavy) cream
10ml/2 tsp chopped fresh tarragon
salt and ground black pepper

For the pastry
175g/6oz/1½ cups plain (all-purpose) flour
5ml/1 tsp soft dark brown sugar
50g/2oz/¼ cup butter
75g/3oz/¾ cup walnuts, ground
15ml/1 tbsp lemon juice
30ml/2 tbsp iced water

1 First make the pastry: sift the flour and 2.5ml/½ tsp salt into a bowl. Add some pepper and the sugar. Rub in the butter until the mixture resembles breadcrumbs, then stir in the ground walnuts. Bind with the lemon juice and iced water. Form the dough into a ball, wrap and chill for 30–40 minutes.

2 Preheat the oven to 190°C/375°F/Gas 5. Roll out the pastry and line a 23cm/9in loose-based metal flan tin (quiche pan). Protect the sides of the pastry with foil, prick the base with a fork and bake for 15 minutes. Remove the foil and bake the flan for a further 5–10 minutes, until just firm to the touch. Reduce the oven temperature to 180°C/350°F/Gas 4.

3 Meanwhile, melt the butter in a pan, add the leeks, cover and cook for 10 minutes. Season with salt and pepper to taste, stir and cook for a further 10 minutes. Cool.

4 Arrange the leeks and slices of Roquefort in the pastry case. Whisk the eggs with the cream and season with black pepper. Beat in the tarragon and pour the mixture into the tart. Bake for 30–40 minutes, until the filling has risen and browned and feels firm when gently touched. Leave to cool for 10 minutes before serving.

Mushroom, Nut & Prune Jalousie

A stunning dish for Sunday lunch, this comprises a nutty filling in a pastry case.

Serves 6
75g/3oz/⅓ cup green lentils, rinsed
5ml/1 tsp vegetable bouillon powder
15ml/1 tbsp sunflower oil
2 large leeks, sliced
2 garlic cloves, chopped
10ml/2 tsp dried mixed herbs
200g/7oz/3 cups field (portabello) mushrooms, finely chopped
75g/3oz/¾ cup chopped mixed nuts
75g/3oz/⅓ cup ready-to-eat stoned (pitted) prunes
25g/1oz/½ cup fresh white breadcrumbs
2 eggs, beaten
2 sheets pre-rolled puff pastry, about 425g/15oz, thawed
flour, for dusting
salt and ground black pepper

1 Put the lentils in a pan and cover with cold water. Bring to the boil, lower the heat and stir in the bouillon powder. Partially cover and simmer for 20 minutes, until the lentils are tender.

2 Heat the oil in a large, heavy frying pan and cook the leeks and garlic for 5 minutes, until softened. Add the herbs and mushrooms and cook for 5 minutes more. Transfer the mixture to a bowl. Stir in the nuts, prunes, breadcrumbs and lentils.

3 Preheat the oven to 220°C/425°F/Gas 7. Add two-thirds of the eggs to the filling mixture and season. Set aside to cool.

4 Meanwhile, unroll one pastry sheet. Cut off and discard a 2.5cm/1in border, then lay it on a dampened baking sheet. Unroll the second sheet, dust lightly with flour, then fold in half lengthways. Make a series of cuts across the fold, 1cm/½in apart, leaving a 2.5cm/1in border around the edge of the pastry.

5 Spoon the filling mixture evenly over the pastry base, leaving a 2.5cm/1in border. Dampen the edges of the base. Open out the folded pastry and lay it over the top of the filling. Trim the edges, then press them together to seal. Crimp the edges. Brush the top with the remaining beaten egg and bake for 25–30 minutes, until golden. Cool slightly before serving.

Cheese & Spinach Flan

This flan freezes well and can be reheated once it has been thawed. It makes an excellent addition to a party buffet table.

Serves 8
225g/8oz/2 cups plain (all-purpose) flour, plus extra for dusting
115g/4oz/ ½ cup butter
2.5ml/ ½ tsp English (hot) mustard powder
2.5ml/ ½ tsp paprika
large pinch of salt
115g/4oz/1 cup grated Cheddar cheese
45–60ml/3–4 tbsp cold water
beaten egg, to glaze

For the filling
450g/1lb frozen spinach
1 onion, finely chopped
pinch of grated nutmeg
225g/8oz/1 cup cottage cheese
2 large (US extra large) eggs
50g/2oz/ ⅔ cup freshly grated Parmesan cheese
150ml/ ¼ pint/ ⅔ cup single (light) cream
salt and ground black pepper

1 Put the flour in a bowl and rub in the butter until the mixture resembles fine breadcrumbs. Stir in the mustard powder, paprika, salt and cheese. Bind to a dough with the cold water. Knead until smooth, wrap and chill for 30 minutes.

2 Make the filling. Put the spinach and onion in a pan, cover and cook gently until the spinach has thawed and the onion is tender. Increase the heat and stir until the mixture is dry. Season with salt, pepper and nutmeg. Spoon the spinach into a bowl and cool slightly. Add the remaining filling ingredients.

3 Preheat the oven to 200°C/400°F/Gas 6. Cut one-third off the pastry and set it aside for the lid. On a lightly floured surface, roll out the rest and line a 23cm/9in loose-based flan tin (quiche pan). Pour the filling into the flan case (pie shell).

4 Roll out the reserved pastry and cut a lid with a lattice pastry cutter. Open the lattice and lay it over the flan. Press the edges together and neaten the joins. Brush the lattice with egg. Bake for 35–40 minutes, or until golden brown. Serve hot or cold.

Wild Mushroom Pie

Wild mushrooms give this pie a really rich flavour.

Serves 6
225g/8oz/2 cups plain (all-purpose) flour
2.5ml/½ tsp salt
115g/4oz/ ½ cup butter
10ml/2 tsp lemon juice
150ml/ ¼ pint/ ⅔ cup iced water
beaten egg, to glaze

For the filling
150g/5oz/ ⅔ cup butter
2 shallots, finely chopped
2 garlic cloves, crushed
450g/1lb/6 cups mixed wild mushrooms, sliced
45ml/3 tbsp chopped fresh parsley
30ml/2 tbsp double (heavy) cream
salt and ground black pepper

1 Sift the flour and salt into a bowl. Rub in half the butter. Cut the remaining butter into cubes and chill. Add the lemon juice to the flour mixture with enough iced water to make a soft dough. Cover and chill for 20 minutes.

2 Roll the pastry out into a rectangle on a lightly floured surface. With a narrow end facing you, mark the dough horizontally into three equal sections. Arrange half the butter cubes over the top two sections of the dough. Fold the bottom section up and the top section down. Seal the edges with a rolling pin. Give the dough a quarter turn and roll it out again. Mark it into thirds and dot with the remaining butter cubes in the same way. Chill for 20 minutes, then repeat the rolling, folding and chilling three times, without the butter.

3 Make the filling. Melt the butter in a pan and cook the shallots and garlic until soft. Add the mushrooms and cook for 35–40 minutes. Stir in the remaining ingredients. Leave to cool. Preheat the oven to 230°C/450°F/Gas 8.

4 Divide the pastry in two. Roll out one half and line a 23cm/9in round tin (pan). Pile the filling into the centre. Roll out the remaining pastry to a round large enough to cover the top. Brush the edge of the case with water and then lay the second round on top. Press the edges together and decorate the top. Brush with egg. Bake for 45 minutes, or until the pastry is golden.

Upside-down Vegetable Tart

This is a Mediterranean variation of the tarte tatin.

Serves 2–4
30ml/2 tbsp sunflower oil
about 25ml/1½ tbsp olive oil
1 aubergine (eggplant),
    sliced lengthways
1 large red (bell) pepper, seeded
    and cut into long strips
5 tomatoes
2 red shallots, finely chopped
1–2 garlic cloves, crushed
150ml/¼ pint/⅔ cup
    white wine
10ml/2 tsp chopped fresh basil
225g/8oz/2 cups long grain rice
40g/1½ oz/⅓ cup pitted black
    olives, chopped
350g/12oz puff pastry, thawed
    if frozen
ground black pepper
lamb's lettuce (corn salad),
    to garnish

1 Cook the rice. Preheat the oven to 190°C/375°F/Gas 5. Heat the sunflower oil with 15ml/1 tbsp of the olive oil in a frying pan and cook the aubergine slices for 4–5 minutes on each side, until golden brown. Lift out and drain on kitchen paper. Add the red pepper to the pan, turning to coat. Cover and sweat over a medium heat for 5–6 minutes, stirring occasionally, until soft and flecked with brown.

2 Slice two of the tomatoes and set them aside. Plunge the remaining tomatoes briefly into boiling water, then peel, cut into quarters and remove the core and seeds. Chop them coarsely.

3 Heat the remaining oil in the pan. Cook the shallots and garlic until softened. Add the chopped tomatoes and cook for 3 minutes. Stir in the wine and basil, with pepper to taste. Bring to the boil, remove from the heat and stir in the rice and olives.

4 Arrange the tomato slices, aubergine slices and peppers in a single layer over the base of a heavy, 30cm/12in shallow ovenproof dish. Spread the rice mixture on top.

5 Roll out the pastry to a round slightly larger than the dish and place on top of the rice, tucking in the overlap. Bake for 25–30 minutes, until risen and golden. Cool slightly, then invert on to a large, warmed serving plate. Garnish with lamb's lettuce.

Greek Picnic Pie

Aubergines layered with spinach, feta and rice make a marvellous filling for a pie.

Serves 6
375g/13oz shortcrust pastry,
    thawed if frozen
45–60ml/3–4 tbsp olive oil
1 large aubergine (eggplant),
    sliced into rounds
1 onion, chopped
1 garlic clove, crushed
175g/6oz spinach
4 eggs
75g/3oz feta cheese
40g/1½oz/½ cup freshly grated
    Parmesan cheese
60ml/4 tbsp natural (plain) yogurt
90ml/6 tbsp creamy milk
225g/8oz/2 cups cooked
    long grain rice
salt and ground black pepper

1 Preheat the oven to 180°C/350°F/Gas 4. Roll out the pastry thinly and line a 25cm/10in flan ring (quiche pan). Prick the pastry all over and bake the unfilled case (pie shell) in the oven for 10–12 minutes, until the pastry is pale golden.

2 Heat 30–45ml/2–3 tbsp of the oil in a frying pan and cook the aubergine slices for 6–8 minutes on each side, until golden. Lift out and drain on kitchen paper.

3 Add the onion and garlic to the oil remaining in the pan and cook gently until soft, adding a little extra oil if necessary.

4 Chop the spinach finely by hand or in a food processor. Beat the eggs in a large mixing bowl, then add the spinach, feta, Parmesan, yogurt, milk and the onion mixture. Season well with salt and pepper and stir thoroughly.

5 Spread the rice in an even layer over the base of the partially cooked pastry case. Reserve a few aubergine slices for the top, and arrange the rest in an even layer over the rice.

6 Spoon the spinach and feta mixture over the aubergines and place the remaining aubergine slices on top. Bake for 30–40 minutes, until lightly browned. Serve the pie warm, or cool completely before transferring to a serving plate or wrapping and packing for a picnic.

Shallot & Garlic Tarte Tatin

Savoury versions of the famous apple tarte tatin have been popular for some years. Here, caramelized shallots are baked beneath a layer of Parmesan pastry.

Serves 4–6

300g/11oz puff pastry, thawed
    if frozen
50g/2oz/¼ cup butter
75g/3oz/1 cup freshly grated
    Parmesan cheese

For the topping

40g/1½oz/3 tbsp butter
500g/1¼lb shallots, peeled but
    left whole
12–16 large garlic cloves, peeled
    but left whole
15ml/1 tbsp golden caster
    (superfine) sugar
15ml/1 tbsp balsamic vinegar
45ml/3 tbsp water
5ml/1 tsp chopped fresh thyme
salt and ground black pepper

1 Roll out the pastry into a rectangle. Spread the butter over it, leaving a 2.5cm/1in border. Sprinkle the Parmesan on top. Fold the bottom third of the pastry up to cover the middle and the top third down. Seal the edges, give a quarter turn and roll out to a rectangle, then fold as before. Chill for 30 minutes.

2 Make the topping. Melt the butter in a 23–25cm/9–10in heavy frying pan that can safely be used in the oven. Add the shallots and garlic and cook until lightly browned all over.

3 Sprinkle the sugar over the top and increase the heat a little. Cook until the sugar begins to caramelize, then turn the shallots and garlic in the buttery juices. Add the vinegar, water and thyme and season to taste. Partially cover the pan and cook for 5–8 minutes, until the garlic cloves are just tender. Cool.

4 Preheat the oven to 190°C/375°F/Gas 5. Roll out the pastry to a round slightly larger than the pan and lay it over the shallots and garlic. Tuck the pastry overlap down inside the pan, then prick the pastry with a sharp knife. Bake the tart for 25–35 minutes, or until it is risen and golden.

5 Cool for 5–10 minutes, then turn the tart out on to a serving platter. Serve, cut in wedges.

Red Onion Tart with a Polenta Crust

Mild red onions go well with Fontina cheese and thyme.

Serves 5–6

60ml/4 tbsp olive oil
1kg/2¼lb red onions, thinly sliced
2–3 garlic cloves, thinly sliced
5ml/1 tsp chopped fresh thyme,
    plus a few whole sprigs
5ml/1 tsp soft dark brown sugar
10ml/2 tsp sherry vinegar
225g/8oz Fontina cheese,
    thinly sliced
salt and ground black pepper

For the pastry

115g/4oz/1 cup plain (all-
    purpose) flour
75g/3oz/¾ cup fine polenta
5ml/1 tsp soft dark brown sugar
5ml/1 tsp chopped fresh thyme
90g/3½oz/7 tbsp butter
1 egg yolk
about 30ml/2 tbsp iced water

1 Make the pastry. Mix the flour and polenta and add salt, pepper, the sugar and thyme. Rub in the butter. Beat the egg yolk with the water and use to bind the pastry. Gather the dough into a ball, wrap and chill for 30–40 minutes.

2 Heat 45ml/3 tbsp of the oil in a frying pan. Add the onions, cover and cook gently, stirring occasionally, for 20–30 minutes. Add the garlic and chopped thyme. Cook, stirring occasionally, for 10 minutes. Increase the heat slightly, then add the sugar and sherry vinegar. Cook, uncovered, for 5–6 minutes more, until the onions start to caramelize slightly. Season to taste. Cool.

3 Preheat the oven to 190°C/375°F/Gas 5. Roll out the pastry thinly and use to line a 25cm/10in loose-based flan tin (quiche pan). Prick the pastry with a fork and support the sides with foil. Bake for 12–15 minutes, until lightly coloured.

4 Spread the onions over the base of the pastry. Add the cheese and most of the thyme sprigs and season. Drizzle over the remaining oil, then bake for 15–20 minutes, until the cheese is bubbling. Serve immediately, garnished with thyme sprigs.

Parsnip & Pecan Gougères

These nutty puffs conceal a sweet parsnip centre.

Makes 18
115g/4oz/ ½ cup butter, plus
    extra for greasing
300ml/ ½ pint/1¼ cups water
75g/3oz/ ⅔ cup plain (all-
    purpose) flour
50g/2oz/ ½ cup wholemeal
    (whole-wheat) flour
3 eggs, beaten
30ml/2 tbsp finely grated
    Cheddar cheese
pinch of cayenne pepper
75g/3oz/ ¾ cup pecan
    nuts, chopped
1 parsnip, cut into 18 x 2cm/
    ¾in pieces
15ml/1 tbsp milk
10ml/2 tsp sesame seeds
fresh watercress sprigs, to garnish
Watercress & Rocket Sauce to
    serve (optional)

1 Preheat the oven to 200°C/400°F/Gas 6. Place the butter and water in a pan. Bring to the boil over a medium heat, then add both the flours. Beat vigorously until the mixture leaves the sides of the pan. Remove from the heat and cool for about 10 minutes. Beat in the eggs, a little at a time, until the mixture is shiny with a soft dropping (pourable) consistency. Beat in the Cheddar, cayenne and pecans.

2 Lightly grease a large baking sheet and drop 18 heaped tablespoons of the mixture on to it. Place a piece of parsnip on each and top with another heaped tablespoon of the mixture.

3 Brush the gougères with a little milk and sprinkle with sesame seeds. Bake for 25–30 minutes, until firm and golden. Garnish with the watercress. Serve with the sauce, if you like.

Cook's Tip
The secret of making successful choux pastry is to let the flour and butter mixture cool before beating in the eggs to prevent them from setting.

Watercress & Rocket Sauce

This fresh-tasting sauce can be served with either of these gougères and is also good with pasta.

Serves 4
150g/5oz watercress, trimmed
150g/5oz rocket (arugula)
175ml/6fl oz/ ¾ cup natural
    (plain) low-fat yogurt
freshly grated nutmeg
salt and ground black pepper

1 Bring a pan of water to the boil and blanch the watercress and rocket for 2–3 minutes. Drain, refresh under cold water, drain again and chop coarsely.
2 Place the watercress and rocket in a blender or food processor with the yogurt and process until smooth. Add a pinch of nutmeg and season to taste with salt and pepper.
3 Just before serving, place in the top of a double boiler or in a heatproof bowl set over a pan of barely simmering water. Heat gently, taking care not to let the sauce curdle.

Mushroom Gougère

A savoury choux pastry ring makes a marvellous main course dish that can be made ahead, then baked when required.

Serves 4
75g/3oz/6 tbsp butter
115g/4oz/1 cup strong white
    bread flour
2.5ml/ ½ tsp salt
200ml/7fl oz/scant 1 cup water
3 eggs, beaten
75g/3oz/ ¾ cup diced
    Gruyère cheese

For the filling
40g/1½oz/3 tbsp butter
1 small onion, sliced
1 carrot, coarsely grated
225g/8oz/3 cups button (white)
    mushrooms, sliced
5ml/1 tsp mild curry paste
25g/1oz/ ¼ cup plain (all-
    purpose) flour
300ml/ ½ pint/1¼ cups milk
30ml/2 tbsp chopped
    fresh parsley
30ml/2 tbsp flaked
    (sliced) almonds
salt and ground black pepper

1 Preheat the oven to 200°C/400°F/Gas 6. Use a little butter to grease a shallow 23cm/9in round ovenproof dish. Sift the flour and salt on to a sheet of greaseproof (waxed) paper.

2 Heat the remaining butter and water in a large pan until the butter just melts, then add all the flour. Beat vigorously until the mixture leaves the sides of the pan and forms a ball.

3 Remove from the heat and cool for 10 minutes. Beat in the eggs, a little at a time, until the mixture is shiny and soft enough to fall gently from a spoon. Stir in the cheese, then spoon the mixture around the sides of the ovenproof dish.

4 Make the filling. Melt the butter in a pan and cook the onion, carrot and mushrooms for 5 minutes. Stir in the curry paste, then the flour. Gradually add the milk, stirring until the mixture boils and thickens. Mix in the parsley, season to taste with salt and pepper, then pour into the centre of the choux ring.

5 Bake for 35–40 minutes, until risen and golden brown, sprinkling on the almonds for the last 5 minutes. Serve immediately, straight from the dish.

SIDE DISHES & SALADS

Don't let side dishes be a mere afterthought. The right accompaniments are what turns an ordinary meal into a truly special one and you should give the same attention and care to your choice of side dishes as you do to the main course. It takes very little extra effort or time to prepare and cook a succulent medley of roasted vegetables, a delicious gratin or a tasty potato combo, yet these will provide that extra special finishing touch. The inspiring recipes in this chapter range from well-known classics, such as Braised Lettuce & Peas and Lyonnaise Potatoes, to unusual and innovative ideas, such as Asparagus with Vermouth Sauce, and Mixed Vegetables with Aromatic Seeds. Use side dishes to enhance the main course – a bright mixture enlivens the appearance of a light-coloured dish, while a crisp gratin provides a superb contrast in textures, served with a casserole or stew.

Salads are a summertime favourite, but often don't live up to our expectations. However, the recipes here will not be disappointing, as they feature an imaginative range of ingredients, from quail's eggs to goat's cheese, combined with a vast variety of salad leaves, fresh vegetables or pasta, tossed in piquant or creamy dressings. Any of the main course salads would be the perfect choice for an al fresco lunch. Other salads may be served as a refreshing side dish at any time of year or could even form a separate, palate-cleansing course, as they often do in France and Italy. Certainly, they are attractive and tasty enough to merit such treatment.

The key to success with both hot side dishes and salads is to use the freshest possible ingredients, preferably on the day of purchase. They will have more colour, flavour and texture, as well as retaining their valuable nutrients. Choose vegetables and salad leaves that are in peak condition for really rewarding results.

Okra with Coriander & Tomatoes

When combined with tomatoes and mild spices, okra makes a very good side dish and is particularly good with potato strudel or a courgette and dill tart.

Serves 4
450g/1lb tomatoes or 400g/14oz
    can chopped tomatoes
450g/1lb fresh okra
45ml/3 tbsp olive oil
2 onions, thinly sliced
10ml/2 tsp coriander
    seeds, crushed
3 garlic cloves, crushed
about 2.5ml/ ½ tsp caster
    (superfine) sugar
finely grated rind and juice
    of 1 lemon
salt and ground black pepper

1 If using fresh tomatoes, cut a cross in the skin at the top of each one with a sharp knife, then plunge them into boiling water for 30 seconds. Drain and refresh in cold water. Peel off the skins and chop the flesh.

2 With a sharp knife, trim off any stalks from the okra and leave the pods whole. Avoid piercing the pods or the sticky juice they contain will leak out.

3 Heat the oil in a large, heavy frying pan. Add the onions with the coriander seeds and cook over a medium heat, stirring occasionally, for 3–4 minutes, until the onions have softened.

4 Add the okra and garlic and cook for 1 minute. Carefully stir in the tomatoes and sugar, without breaking up the okra, then lower the heat and simmer gently for about 20 minutes, or until the okra is tender, stirring once or twice.

5 Stir in the lemon rind and juice. Season to taste with salt and pepper. Taste the mixture and add a little more sugar, if necessary. Transfer to a warmed serving dish and serve immediately. Alternatively, set aside to cool and then serve at room temperature.

Braised Lettuce & Peas

This dish is based on the traditional French way of braising peas with lettuce and spring onions in butter.

Serves 4
50g/2oz/ ¼ cup butter
4 Little Gem (Bibb) lettuces,
    halved lengthways
2 bunches of spring onions
    (scallions), trimmed

5ml/1 tsp caster (superfine) sugar
400g/14oz/3½ cups shelled peas
    (about 1kg/2¼lb in pods)
4 fresh mint sprigs
120ml/4fl oz/ ½ cup
    vegetable stock
15ml/1 tbsp fresh mint leaves
salt and ground black pepper

1 Melt half the butter in a heavy pan over a low heat. Add the lettuces and spring onions. Turn the vegetables in the butter, then sprinkle in the sugar, 2.5ml/ ½ tsp salt and plenty of black pepper. Cover, and cook very gently for 5 minutes, stirring once.

2 Add the peas and mint sprigs. Turn the peas in the buttery juices and pour in the stock, then cover and cook over a gentle heat for 5 minutes more. Uncover and increase the heat to reduce the liquid to a few tablespoons.

3 Stir in the remaining butter. Transfer to a warmed serving dish and sprinkle with the mint leaves. Serve immediately.

Variations
• Braise about eight baby carrots with the lettuce.
• Use 1 lettuce, shredding it coarsely, and omit the mint. Towards the end of cooking, stir in about 150g/5oz rocket (arugula) (preferably the stronger-flavoured wild rocket) and cook briefly until the leaves are just wilted.
• Any of the smaller cos or romaine lettuces, such as Sucrine and Winter Density, would work well in this recipe. Equally, you could use shredded Webb's Wonder leaves.
• For a different flavour, omit the mint and season with freshly grated nutmeg to taste.

Broad Beans with Cream

Tiny new broad beans can be eaten raw with a little salt, just like radishes. More mature beans taste wonderful when cooked and skinned to reveal the bright green kernel inside.

Serves 4–6
450g/1lb shelled broad (fava)
   beans (from about 2kg/4½lb
   beans in the pod)
90ml/6 tbsp crème fraîche or
   whipping cream
salt and ground black pepper
finely chopped chives, to garnish

1 Bring a large pan of lightly salted water to the boil over a medium heat. Add the beans. Bring the water back to the boil, then lower the heat slightly and cook the beans gently for about 8 minutes, until just tender. Drain and rinse under cold water, then drain again.

2 To remove the skins, make a slit along one side of each bean with the tip of a sharp knife and then gently squeeze out the kernel with your fingers.

3 Put the skinned beans in a pan with the crème fraîche or whipping cream, season with salt and pepper to taste, cover and heat through gently. Transfer to a warmed serving dish, sprinkle with the chopped chives and serve immediately.

> **Variation**
> If you can find them, fresh flageolet (small navy) or lima beans may be served in the same way.

Asparagus with Vermouth Sauce

Coating grilled young asparagus spears with a vermouth and parsley sauce creates a sensational dish.

Serves 4
20 asparagus spears
5ml/1 tsp olive oil
50g/2oz/⅔ cup freshly grated
   Parmesan cheese
salt and ground black pepper

For the sauce
45ml/3 tbsp dry white vermouth
250ml/8fl oz/1 cup well-flavoured
   vegetable stock
15ml/1 tbsp chopped
   fresh parsley
25g/1oz/2 tbsp chilled
   butter, cubed

1 Brush the asparagus spears with olive oil and seasoning. Place on a grill (broiler) rack, sprinkle with the Parmesan and grill (broil) slowly under moderate heat, until the asparagus is just tender when pierced with the tip of a knife and lightly charred.
2 Meanwhile, make the sauce. Pour the vermouth and stock into a pan. Boil over a high heat until reduced by half. Stir in the parsley and season with salt and pepper.
3 Lower the heat and stir in the chilled butter cubes, two at a time. Continue to stir over a gentle heat until all the butter has melted and the sauce has thickened. Arrange the asparagus spears in a serving dish, pour the sauce over and serve.

Runner Beans with Garlic

Flageolet beans and garlic add a distinct French flavour to this simple side dish.

Serves 4
225g/8oz/1¼ cups dried
   flageolet (small navy) beans,
   soaked overnight and drained
15ml/1 tbsp olive oil
25g/1oz/2 tbsp butter
1 onion, finely chopped

1–2 garlic cloves, crushed
3–4 tomatoes, peeled
   and chopped
350g/12oz green beans, sliced
150ml/¼ pint/⅔ cup
   white wine
150ml/¼ pint/⅔ cup
   vegetable stock
30ml/2 tbsp chopped
   fresh parsley
salt and ground black pepper

1 Place the flageolet beans in a large pan of water, bring to the boil over a medium heat, then lower the heat and simmer for 45 minutes–1 hour, until tender. Drain thoroughly and set aside.

2 Heat the oil and butter in a large, heavy frying pan. Add the onion and garlic and cook over a low heat, stirring occasionally, for 3–4 minutes, until soft.

3 Add the chopped tomatoes to the pan and cook over a gentle heat until they are soft.

4 Stir the flageolet beans into the onion and tomato mixture, then add the green beans, wine and stock and season with a little salt. Stir well. Cover and simmer for 5–10 minutes, until the green beans are tender.

5 Increase the heat to medium to reduce the liquid, then stir in the chopped parsley. Check the seasoning, adding a little more salt, if necessary, and pepper. Transfer to a warmed serving dish and serve immediately.

> **Cook's Tip**
> Flageolets are also known as green haricot beans.

Radicchio & Chicory Gratin

Creamy béchamel sauce is the perfect foil for these bitter-tasting leaves.

Serves 4
oil, for greasing
2 heads radicchio
2 heads chicory (Belgian endive)
4 pieces of sun-dried tomatoes
   in oil, drained and
   coarsely chopped
30ml/2 tbsp oil from the sun-
   dried tomato jar
25g/1oz/2 tbsp butter
15ml/1 tbsp plain (all-
   purpose) flour
250ml/8fl oz/1 cup milk
pinch of freshly grated nutmeg
50g/2oz/ ½ cup grated
   Emmenthal cheese
salt and ground black pepper
chopped fresh parsley, to garnish

1 Preheat the oven to 180°C/350°F/Gas 4. Grease a 1.2 litre/ 2 pint/5 cup ovenproof dish. Trim the radicchio and chicory and pull away and discard any damaged or wilted leaves. Quarter them lengthways and arrange them in the dish.

2 Sprinkle over the sun-dried tomatoes and brush the leaves liberally with the oil from the jar. Sprinkle with salt and pepper and cover with foil. Bake for 15 minutes, then remove the foil and bake for 10 minutes more, until the vegetables are soft.

3 Meanwhile, make the sauce. Melt the butter in a small pan, stir in the flour and cook for 1 minute. Gradually add the milk, whisking until the sauce boils and thickens. Lower the heat and simmer for 2–3 minutes. Season to taste and add the nutmeg.

4 Pour the sauce over the vegetables and sprinkle with the cheese. Bake for 20 minutes more, until the topping is golden. Serve immediately, garnished with parsley.

Cook's Tip
In Italy radicchio and chicory (Belgian endive) are often cooked on a barbecue. Prepare the vegetables as above and brush with olive oil. Place cut side down on the grill for 7–10 minutes, until browned. Turn and cook until the other side is browned.

Mixed Vegetables with Aromatic Seeds

A tantalizing aroma is the first indication of how tasty this vegetable medley will be. Fresh ginger and three different types of seeds create a wonderful flavour.

Serves 4–6
675g/1½lb small new potatoes
1 small cauliflower
175g/6oz green beans
115g/4oz/1 cup frozen peas
a small piece of fresh root ginger
30ml/2 tbsp sunflower oil
10ml/2 tsp cumin seeds
10ml/2 tsp black mustard seeds
30ml/2 tbsp sesame seeds
juice of 1 lemon
salt and ground black pepper

1 Scrub the potatoes but do not peel them. Cut the cauliflower into small florets, then trim and halve the green beans.

2 Cook the vegetables in separate pans of lightly salted boiling water until tender, allowing 15–20 minutes for the potatoes, 8–10 minutes for the cauliflower and 4–5 minutes for the beans and peas. Drain thoroughly.

3 Using a small, sharp knife, peel and finely chop the ginger.

4 Heat the oil in a wide, shallow pan. Add the ginger and seeds. Cover the pan and cook until the seeds start to pop.

5 Add the cooked vegetables and toss over the heat for another 2–3 minutes. Sprinkle over the lemon juice and season with pepper. Serve immediately.

Cook's Tip
Other vegetables could be used, such as courgettes (zucchini), leeks or broccoli. Buy whatever looks freshest and do not store vegetables for long periods, as their vitamin content, flavour and texture will deteriorate.

Baked Peppers & Tomatoes

The juices from this vegetable medley are absolutely delicious, so serve it with a pasta or rice dish or just crusty bread to soak them up.

Serves 8
2 red (bell) peppers, seeded
2 yellow (bell) peppers, seeded
1 red onion, sliced
2 garlic cloves, halved
6 plum tomatoes, quartered
50g/2oz/ 1/4 cup black olives
5ml/1 tsp light brown sugar
45ml/3 tbsp sherry
3–4 fresh rosemary sprigs
30ml/2 tbsp olive oil
salt and ground black pepper

1 Preheat the oven to 200°C/400°F/Gas 6. Cut each pepper into 12 strips and place them in a large roasting pan. Add the onion, garlic, tomatoes and olives.

2 Sprinkle over the sugar, then drizzle over the sherry. Season well, cover with foil and bake for 45 minutes.

3 Remove the foil from the pan and stir the mixture well. Add the rosemary sprigs.

4 Drizzle over the olive oil. Return the pan to the oven and roast for 30 minutes more, until the vegetables are tender. Serve hot.

> **Cook's Tip**
> For the best flavour, buy tomatoes on the vine, if possible.

> **Variation**
> Use four or five well-flavoured beefsteak tomatoes instead of plum tomatoes, if you like. Cut them into thick wedges instead of quarters.

Celeriac Gratin

It may not look very handsome, but celeriac has a delicious sweet and nutty flavour, which is accentuated in this dish by the addition of Emmenthal cheese.

Serves 4
juice of 1/2 lemon
450g/1lb celeriac
25g/1oz/2 tbsp butter
1 small onion, finely chopped
30ml/2 tbsp plain (all-purpose) flour
300ml/ 1/2 pint/1 1/4 cups milk
25g/1oz/1/4 cup grated Emmenthal cheese
15ml/1 tbsp capers, rinsed and drained
salt and cayenne pepper

1 Preheat the oven to 190°C/375°F/Gas 5. Fill a pan with water and add the lemon juice. Peel the celeriac and cut it into 5mm/ 1/4in slices, immediately adding them to the pan of acidulated water. This prevents them from discolouring.

2 Bring the water to the boil, then lower the heat and simmer the celeriac for 10–12 minutes, until just tender. Drain the celeriac and arrange the slices, overlapping them slightly, in a shallow ovenproof dish.

3 Melt the butter in a small pan. Add the onion and cook over a low heat, stirring occasionally, for 5 minutes, until soft but not browned. Stir in the flour, cook for 1 minute and then gradually add the milk, stirring constantly until the mixture thickens to make a smooth sauce.

4 Stir in the grated cheese and capers and season with salt and cayenne to taste. Pour the mixture over the celeriac. Bake for 15–20 minutes, until the top is golden brown.

> **Variation**
> For a less strongly flavoured dish, alternate the layers of celeriac with potato. Slice the potato, cook until almost tender, then drain well before assembling the dish.

Potato Pan Gratin

Baked potatoes layered with mustard butter are perfect to serve with a green salad for supper, or as an accompaniment to a vegetable or nut roast.

Serves 4

4 large potatoes, total weight about 1kg/2¼ lb
25g/1oz/2 tbsp butter
15ml/1 tbsp olive oil
2 large garlic cloves, crushed
30ml/2 tbsp plain or herbed Dijon mustard
15ml/1 tbsp lemon juice
15ml/1 tbsp fresh thyme leaves, plus extra to garnish
60ml/4 tbsp well-flavoured vegetable stock
salt and ground black pepper

1 Peel the potatoes and slice them thinly, using a knife or the slicing attachment on a food processor. Place the slices in a bowl of cold water to prevent them from discolouring.

2 Preheat the oven to 200°C/400°F/Gas 6. Heat the butter and oil in a deep frying pan that can safely be used in the oven. Add the garlic and cook gently for 3 minutes, until light golden, stirring constantly. Stir in the mustard, lemon juice and thyme. Remove from the heat and pour into a jug (pitcher).

3 Drain the potatoes and pat them dry with kitchen paper. Place a layer of potatoes in the frying pan, season and pour over one-third of the butter mixture. Place another layer of potatoes on top, season, and pour over another third of the butter mixture. Arrange a final layer of potatoes on top, pour over the remainder of the butter mixture and then the stock. Season and sprinkle with the extra thyme.

4 Cover with baking parchment and bake for 1 hour. Remove the parchment and bake for 15 minutes more, until golden.

> **Variation**
> *Any root vegetables can be used: try celery sticks, parsnips, carrots or a mixture.*

Lyonnaise Potatoes

Two simple ingredients are prepared separately and then tossed together to create the perfect combination. These potatoes go very well with grilled beefsteak tomatoes and lightly cooked green beans.

Serves 6

900g/2lb floury potatoes, scrubbed but not peeled
vegetable oil, for shallow frying
25g/1oz/2 tbsp butter
15ml/1 tbsp olive oil
2 medium onions, sliced into rings
sea salt
15ml/1 tbsp chopped fresh parsley

1 Bring a large pan of lightly salted water to the boil and cook the potatoes for 10 minutes. Drain them in a colander and leave to cool slightly. When the potatoes are cool enough to handle, peel them and slice them thinly.

2 Heat the vegetable oil in a large, heavy pan. Add half the potato slices and cook over a low heat, turning occasionally, for about 10 minutes, until crisp. Remove from the pan with a slotted spoon and drain on kitchen paper. Set aside and keep hot while you cook the remaining potato slices.

3 Meanwhile, melt the butter with the olive oil in a frying pan. Add the onions and cook over a low heat, stirring occasionally, for about 10 minutes, until golden. Drain on kitchen paper.

4 Remove the second batch of potato slices with a slotted spoon and drain on kitchen paper. Mix the two batches together in a warmed serving dish, toss with sea salt and carefully mix with the onions. Sprinkle with the parsley and serve.

> **Variation**
> *For garlic-flavoured Lyonnaise potatoes, add about six unpeeled garlic cloves when you par-boil the potatoes in step 1. Then either leave them whole or squeeze out the flesh and spread it over the potatoes.*

Swiss Soufflé Potatoes

A fabulous combination of rich and satisfying ingredients – cheese, eggs, cream, butter and potatoes. This is perfect for cold-weather entertaining.

Serves 4
4 floury baking potatoes, total
* weight about 900g/2lb*
115g/4oz/1 cup grated
* Gruyère cheese*
115g/4oz/ ¹/₂ cup herb butter
60ml/4 tbsp double
* (heavy) cream*
2 eggs, separated
salt and ground black pepper
chopped fresh chives, to garnish
Mayonnaise, to serve (optional)

1 Preheat the oven to 220°C/425°F/Gas 7. Prick the potatoes with a fork. Bake for 1–1¹/₂ hours, until tender. Remove from the oven and reduce the temperature to 180°C/350°F/Gas 4.

2 Cut each potato in half and scoop out the flesh into a bowl. Place the potato shells on a baking sheet and return them to the oven to crisp up while you are making the filling.

3 Mash the potato flesh, then add the Gruyère, herb butter, cream and egg yolks. Beat well until smooth, then taste and add salt and pepper if necessary.

4 Whisk the egg whites to stiff peaks, then carefully fold them into the potato mixture. Pile the mixture into the potato shells and bake for 20–25 minutes, until risen and golden brown.

5 Transfer the potatoes to a warm serving dish, garnish with chives and serve with mayonnaise, if you like.

> **Cook's Tip**
> *To make the herb butter, mix 45ml/3 tbsp finely chopped fresh parsley and 10ml/2 tsp finely chopped fresh dill with 115g/4oz/ ¹/₂ cup softened butter. Season with a little salt.*

Caribbean Roasted Sweet Potatoes, Onions & Beetroot

An aromatic coconut, ginger and garlic paste makes this colourful medley of root vegetables truly memorable and a veritable feast.

Serves 4
30ml/2 tbsp groundnut
* (peanut) oil*
450g/1lb sweet potatoes, peeled
* and cut into thick strips*
4 freshly cooked beetroot (beets),
* peeled and cut into wedges*
450g/1lb small red or yellow
* onions, halved*
5ml/1 tsp coriander seeds,
* lightly crushed*
3–4 small whole fresh red chillies

salt and ground black pepper
chopped fresh coriander (cilantro),
* to garnish*

For the paste
2 large garlic cloves, chopped
1–2 fresh green chillies, seeded
* and chopped*
15ml/1 tbsp chopped fresh
* root ginger*
45ml/3 tbsp chopped fresh
* coriander (cilantro)*
76ml/5 tbsp coconut milk
30ml/2 tbsp groundnut
* (peanut) oil*
grated rind of ¹/₂ lime
2.5ml/ ¹/₂ tsp light muscovado
* (molasses) sugar*

1 Preheat the oven to 200°C/400°F/Gas 6. Make the paste. Process the garlic, chillies, ginger, coriander and coconut milk in a food processor or blender. Scrape the paste into a small bowl and beat in the oil, lime rind and muscovado sugar.

2 Heat the oil in a roasting pan in the oven for 5 minutes. Add the sweet potatoes, beetroot, onions and coriander seeds, tossing them in the hot oil. Roast for 10 minutes.

3 Stir in the paste and the red chillies. Season to taste and toss the vegetables to coat them thoroughly with the paste.

4 Roast the vegetables for a further 25–35 minutes, or until the sweet potatoes and onions are fully cooked and tender. Stir occasionally to prevent the paste from sticking to the pan. Transfer to a warmed platter and serve immediately, sprinkled with a little chopped fresh coriander.

Marquis Potatoes

Swirled potato nests filled with a tangy tomato mixture look wonderfully appetizing and taste superb. As a side dish, this recipe will serve six, but could also make a tasty lunch for two or three people.

Makes 6 nests

4 large floury potatoes, total
  weight about 900g/2lb
15ml/1 tbsp olive oil, plus extra
  for greasing
2 shallots, finely chopped
450g/1lb ripe tomatoes, peeled,
  seeded and diced
25g/1oz/2 tbsp butter
60ml/4 tbsp milk
3 egg yolks
salt and ground black pepper
chopped fresh parsley, to garnish

1 Peel the potatoes and cut them into small chunks. Put them in a pan of cold water. Add salt, bring to the boil and cook for 20 minutes, or until very tender.

2 Heat the olive oil in a large frying pan. Add the shallots and cook, stirring constantly, for 2 minutes.

3 Add the diced tomatoes and cook over a low heat, stirring occasionally, for 10 minutes more, until all the moisture has evaporated. Keep warm over a low heat.

4 Drain the potatoes in a colander, then return them to the pan so that they can dry off. Cool slightly, then mash with the butter, the milk and two of the egg yolks. Season to taste with salt and pepper.

5 Preheat the grill (broiler) and grease a baking sheet. Spoon the potato mixture into a piping (pastry) bag fitted with a medium star nozzle. Pipe six oval nests on to the baking sheet. Beat the remaining egg yolk with a little water and carefully brush over the potato. Grill (broil) for 5 minutes, until golden.

6 Spoon the tomato mixture inside the nests and top with a little parsley. Serve them immediately.

Gratin Dauphinois

This popular baked dish is a delicious alternative to traditional roast potatoes, particularly as it needs no last-minute attention.

Serves 8

butter, for greasing
1.6kg/3½lb potatoes
2–3 garlic cloves, crushed
115g/4oz/1 cup grated
  Cheddar cheese
2.5ml/½ tsp freshly
  grated nutmeg
600ml/1 pint/2½ cups milk
300ml/½ pint/1¼ cups single
  (light) cream
2 large (US extra large)
  eggs, beaten
salt and ground black pepper

1 Preheat the oven to 180°C/350°F/Gas 4. Generously grease a 2.4 litre/4 pint/10 cup shallow ovenproof dish with butter. Peel the potatoes and slice them thinly.

2 Layer the potatoes in the dish, with the garlic and two-thirds of the grated cheese. Season each layer with salt and pepper to taste and a little grated nutmeg.

3 Whisk the milk, cream and eggs in a jug (pitcher), then pour the mixture over the potatoes. If necessary, prick the layered potatoes with a skewer so that the liquid goes all the way to the base of the dish.

4 Sprinkle the remaining grated cheese on top and bake for 45–50 minutes, or until golden brown. Test the potatoes with a sharp knife; they should be very tender. Serve immediately.

Variations
• For a lower-fat version, substitute skimmed milk for the full-cream (whole) milk. Omit the cheese and cream and use 150g/5oz fromage blanc instead.
• For gratin savoyarde, omit the milk, cream and eggs. Substitute Beaufort cheese for the Cheddar. Layer the potatoes with the cheese and knobs (pats) of butter, then pour in 900ml/1½ pints/3¾ cups vegetable stock. Bake as above.

Springtime Salad with Quail's Eggs

Enjoy some of the best early season garden vegetables in this crunchy green salad. Quail's eggs add a touch of sophistication and elegance.

Serves 4
175g/6oz broad (fava) beans
175g/6oz fresh peas
175g/6oz asparagus
175g/6oz very small new
 potatoes, scrubbed
45ml/3 tbsp good lemon
 mayonnaise (see Cook's Tip)
45ml/3 tbsp sour cream or
 crème fraîche
1/2 bunch of fresh mint, chopped,
 plus whole leaves for garnishing
8 quail's eggs, soft-boiled
 and peeled
salt and ground black pepper

1 Cook the broad beans, peas, asparagus and new potatoes in separate pans of lightly salted boiling water until just tender. Drain, refresh under cold water and drain again.

2 When the vegetables are cold, mix them lightly in a bowl.

3 Mix the mayonnaise with the sour cream or crème fraîche and chopped mint in a jug (pitcher). Season to taste.

4 Pour the dressing over the salad and toss to coat. Add the quail's eggs and whole mint leaves and toss very gently to mix. Serve immediately.

Cook's Tip
To make your own lemon mayonnaise, combine two egg yolks, 5ml/1 tsp Dijon mustard, and the grated rind and juice of half a lemon in a blender or food processor. Add salt and pepper to taste. Process to combine. With the motor running, add about 250ml/8fl oz/1 cup mild olive oil (or a mixture of olive oil and sunflower oil) through the lid or feeder tube, until the mixture emulsifies. Trickle the oil in at first, then add it in a steady stream. For a glossy mayonnaise, beat in about 15ml/1 tbsp boiling water at the end.

Warm Dressed Salad with Poached Eggs

Soft poached eggs, hot croûtons and cool, crisp salad leaves with a warm dressing make a lively and unusual combination.

Serves 2
1/2 small loaf Granary (multi-
 grain) bread
45ml/3 tbsp walnut oil
2 eggs
115g/4oz mixed salad leaves
45ml/3 tbsp extra virgin olive oil
2 garlic cloves, crushed
15ml/1 tbsp balsamic or
 sherry vinegar
50g/2oz piece of Parmesan
 cheese, shaved
ground black pepper (optional)

1 Carefully cut off the crust from the Granary loaf and discard it. Cut the bread into 2.5cm/1in cubes.

2 Heat the walnut oil in a large, heavy frying pan. Add the bread cubes and cook over a low heat for about 5 minutes, turning and tossing the cubes occasionally, until they are crisp and golden brown all over.

3 Bring a pan of water to the boil. Break each egg into a jug (pitcher), one at a time, and carefully slide each one into the water. Gently poach the eggs over a low heat for about 4 minutes, until lightly cooked and the whites have just set.

4 Meanwhile, divide the salad leaves among two plates. Arrange the croûtons over the leaves.

5 Wipe the frying pan clean with kitchen paper. Heat the olive oil in the pan, add the garlic and vinegar and cook over a high heat for 1 minute. Pour the warm dressing over the salad on each plate.

6 Lift out each poached egg, in turn, with a slotted spoon and place one on top of each of the salads. Top with thin shavings of Parmesan and a little freshly ground black pepper, if you like. Serve immediately.

Avocado, Red Onion & Spinach Salad with Polenta Croûtons

The simple lemon dressing gives a sharp tang to this sophisticated salad, while the croûtons, with their crunchy golden exterior and soft centre, add a contrast.

Serves 4
1 large red onion, cut into wedges
300g/11oz ready-made polenta,
   cut into 1cm/ ½in cubes

olive oil, for brushing
225g/8oz baby spinach leaves
1 avocado
5ml/1 tsp lemon juice

For the dressing
60ml/4 tbsp extra virgin olive oil
juice of ½ lemon
salt and ground black pepper

1 Preheat the oven to 200°C/400°F/Gas 6. Place the onion wedges and polenta cubes on a lightly oiled baking sheet and bake for 25 minutes, or until the onion is tender and the polenta is crisp and golden, turning everything frequently to prevent sticking. Leave to cool slightly.

2 Meanwhile, make the dressing. Place the olive oil and lemon juice in a screw-top jar. Add salt and pepper to taste, close the jar tightly and shake vigorously to combine.

3 Place the spinach in a serving bowl. Peel, stone (pit) and slice the avocado, then toss the slices in the lemon juice to prevent discoloration. Add them to the spinach with the onions.

4 Pour the dressing over the salad and toss gently. Sprinkle the polenta croûtons on top or hand them separately.

Cook's Tip
If you can't find ready-made polenta, you can make your own using instant polenta grains. Simply cook 115g/4oz/1 cup according to the instructions on the packet, then pour into a tray and leave to cool and set.

Watercress, Pear, Walnut & Roquefort Salad

Sharp-tasting blue Roquefort and peppery leaves are complemented in this salad by sweet fruit and crunchy nuts.

Serves 4
75g/3oz/ ¾ cup shelled
   walnuts, halved
2 red Williams pears
15ml/1 tbsp lemon juice

1 large bunch of watercress,
   about 150g/5oz, tough
   stalks removed
200g/7oz Roquefort cheese, cut
   into chunks

For the dressing
45ml/3 tbsp extra virgin olive oil
30ml/2 tbsp lemon juice
2.5ml/ ½ tsp clear honey
5ml/1 tsp Dijon mustard
salt and ground black pepper

1 Toast the walnuts in a dry frying pan over a low heat for about 2 minutes, until golden, tossing frequently to prevent them from burning.

2 Meanwhile, make the dressing. Put the olive oil, lemon juice, honey and mustard into a screw-top jar and season to taste with salt and pepper. Close the lid tightly and shake vigorously until thoroughly combined.

3 Core and slice the pears then toss them in the lemon juice to prevent them from discolouring. Place the slices in a bowl and add the watercress, walnuts and Roquefort. Pour the dressing over the salad, toss well and serve immediately.

Cook's Tip
For a special dinner party, fan the pears on a bed of the dressed watercress. Cut the pears in half, remove the cores, then, keeping them intact at the top, slice them lengthways. Brush them with lemon juice to prevent discoloration, then place one half, cut side down, on each salad. Press down gently to fan the slices. Sprinkle the toasted walnuts over.

Sweet-&-sour Artichoke Salad

This Italian salad combines spring vegetables with a deliciously piquant sauce called *agrodolce*.

Serves 4
juice of 1 lemon
6 small globe artichokes
30ml/2 tbsp olive oil
2 medium onions,
   coarsely chopped
175g/6oz/1 cup shelled fresh or
   frozen broad (fava) beans

300ml/½ pint/1¼ cups water
175g/6oz/1½ cups shelled fresh
   or frozen peas
salt and ground black pepper
fresh mint leaves, to garnish

For the sauce
120ml/4fl oz/½ cup white
   wine vinegar
15ml/1 tbsp caster
   (superfine) sugar
a handful of fresh mint leaves,
   coarsely torn

1 Fill a bowl with cold water and add the lemon juice. Peel the outer leaves from the artichokes and discard them. Cut the artichokes into quarters and place them in the bowl of acidulated water to prevent them from discolouring.

2 Heat the oil in a large, heavy pan. Add the onions and cook over a low heat, stirring occasionally, until they are golden.

3 Stir in the beans, then drain the artichokes and add them to the pan. Pour in the measured water. Bring the water to the boil, lower the heat, cover and cook for 10–15 minutes.

4 Add the peas, season to taste with salt and pepper and cook for 5 minutes more, stirring occasionally, until the vegetables are tender. Drain them thoroughly, place them in a bowl, leave to cool, then cover and chill.

5 Make the sauce. Mix all the ingredients in a small pan. Heat gently for 2–3 minutes, until the sugar has dissolved. Simmer for about another 5 minutes, stirring occasionally. Remove from the heat and leave to cool.

6 To serve, drizzle the sauce over the vegetables and garnish with the fresh mint leaves.

Beetroot & Red Onion Salad

This salad looks especially attractive when it is made with a mixture of red and yellow beetroot.

Serves 6
500g/1¼lb small beetroot (beets)
75ml/5 tbsp water
60ml/4 tbsp olive oil
90g/3½ oz/scant 1 cup
   walnut halves
5ml/1 tsp caster (superfine)
   sugar, plus a little extra for
   the dressing
30ml/2 tbsp walnut oil

15ml/1 tbsp sherry vinegar
5ml/1 tsp soy sauce
5ml/1 tsp grated orange rind
2.5ml/ ½ tsp ground roasted
   coriander seeds
5–10ml/1–2 tsp orange juice
1 red onion, halved and very
   thinly sliced
15–30ml/1–2 tbsp chopped
   fresh fennel
75g/3oz watercress or
   mizuna leaves
handful of baby red chard or
   beetroot (beet) leaves (optional)
salt and ground black pepper

1 Preheat the oven to 180°C/350°F/Gas 4. Place the beetroot in an ovenproof dish in a single layer and add the water. Cover tightly and bake for 1–1½ hours, or until they are just tender.

2 Cool, then peel the beetroot. Slice or cut them into strips and toss with 15ml/1 tbsp of the olive oil in a bowl. Set aside.

3 Heat 15ml/1 tbsp of the remaining olive oil in a small frying pan. Cook the walnuts until starting to brown. Add the sugar and cook, stirring, until starting to caramelize. Season with pepper and 2.5ml/ ½ tsp salt, then tip them on to a plate.

4 In a jug (pitcher), whisk together the remaining olive oil, the walnut oil, sherry vinegar, soy sauce, orange rind and coriander seeds. Season with salt and pepper and add a pinch of caster sugar. Whisk in orange juice to taste.

5 Separate the red onion slices into half-rings and add them to the beetroot. Pour over the dressing and toss well. When ready to serve, toss the salad with the fennel, watercress or mizuna and red chard or beetroot leaves, if using. Transfer to individual bowls or plates and sprinkle with the caramelized nuts.

Leek & Grilled Pepper Salad with Goat's Cheese

This is a perfect dish for entertaining, as the salad actually benefits from being made in advance.

Serves 6
4 x 1cm/ ½in slices goat's cheese
75g/3oz/ 1 cup fine dry
  white breadcrumbs
675g/1½ lb young leeks
15ml/1 tbsp olive oil
2 large red (bell) peppers, halved
  and seeded

few fresh thyme sprigs, chopped
vegetable oil, for shallow frying
45ml/3 tbsp chopped fresh flat
  leaf parsley
salt and ground black pepper

For the dressing
75ml/5 tbsp extra virgin olive oil
1 small garlic clove,
  finely chopped
5ml/1 tsp Dijon mustard
15ml/1 tbsp red wine vinegar

1 Roll the cheese slices in the breadcrumbs, pressing them in so that the cheese is well coated. Chill the cheese for 1 hour.

2 Preheat the grill (broiler). Bring a pan of lightly salted water to the boil and cook the leeks for 3–4 minutes. Drain, cut into 10cm/4in lengths and place in a bowl. Add the olive oil, toss to coat, then season to taste. Place the leeks on a grill rack and grill (broil) for 3–4 minutes on each side.

3 Set the leeks aside. Place the peppers on the grill rack, skin side up, and grill until blackened and blistered. Place them in a bowl, cover with crumpled kitchen paper and leave for 10 minutes. Rub off the skin and cut the flesh into strips. Place in a bowl and add the leeks, thyme and a little pepper.

4 Make the dressing by shaking all the ingredients together in a jar, adding seasoning to taste. Pour the dressing over the leek mixture, cover and chill for several hours.

5 Heat a little oil and fry the cheese until golden on both sides. Drain and cool, then cut into bitesize pieces. Toss the cheese and parsley into the salad and serve at room temperature.

Butternut Salad with Feta Cheese

This is especially good served with a grain or starchy salad, based on rice or couscous. The salad is best served warm or at room temperature, rather than chilled.

Serves 4–6
75ml/5 tbsp olive oil
15ml/1 tbsp balsamic vinegar,
  plus a little extra if needed
15ml/1 tbsp sweet soy sauce
  (kecap manis)

350g/12oz shallots, peeled but
  left whole
3 fresh red chillies, chopped
1 butternut squash, peeled,
  seeded and cut into chunks
5ml/1 tsp finely chopped
  fresh thyme
15g/ ½ oz/ ½ cup flat
  leaf parsley
1 small garlic clove,
  finely chopped
75g/3oz/¾ cup walnuts, chopped
150g/5oz feta cheese
salt and ground black pepper

1 Preheat the oven to 200°C/400°F/Gas 6. Put the olive oil, balsamic vinegar and soy sauce in a large bowl and beat until thoroughly combined.

2 Toss the shallots and two of the chillies in the oil mixture and tip into a large, shallow roasting pan. Roast, uncovered, for about 25 minutes, stirring once or twice.

3 Add the butternut squash and roast for 35–40 minutes more, stirring once, until the squash is tender and browned. Remove from the oven, stir in the chopped thyme and set the vegetables aside to cool.

4 Chop the parsley and garlic together and mix with the walnuts. Seed and finely chop the remaining chilli.

5 Stir the parsley, garlic and walnut mixture into the cooled vegetables. Add the remaining chopped chilli. Taste and season with salt and pepper, if necessary, and add a little extra balsamic vinegar. Crumble the feta and add it to the salad.

6 Transfer to a serving dish and serve immediately, at room temperature, rather than chilled.

Roasted Plum Tomato & Rocket Salad

This is a good side salad to accompany a cheese flan or a fresh herb pizza.

Serves 4

450g/1lb ripe baby Italian plum
   tomatoes, halved lengthways
75ml/5 tbsp extra virgin olive oil
2 garlic cloves, cut into thin slivers
225g/8oz/2 cups dried
   pasta shapes
30ml/2 tbsp balsamic vinegar
2 pieces sun-dried tomato in olive
   oil, drained and chopped
large pinch of granulated sugar
1 handful rocket (arugula) leaves
salt and ground black pepper

1 Preheat the oven to 190°C/375°F/Gas 5. Arrange the halved tomatoes, cut side up, in a roasting pan. Drizzle 30ml/ 2 tbsp of the oil over them and sprinkle with the slivers of garlic and salt and pepper to taste. Roast for 20 minutes, turning once.

2 Meanwhile, bring a large pan of lightly salted water to the boil and cook the pasta until it is *al dente*.

3 Put the remaining oil in a large bowl with the vinegar, sun-dried tomatoes and sugar with salt and pepper to taste.

4 Drain the pasta, add it to the bowl of dressing and toss to mix. Add the roasted tomatoes and mix gently.

5 Just before serving, add the rocket leaves, toss lightly and taste for seasoning. Serve at room temperature or chilled.

> **Variations**
> • If you are in a hurry and don't have time to roast the tomatoes, you can make the salad with halved raw tomatoes instead, but make sure that they are really ripe.
> • If you like, add 150g/5oz mozzarella cheese, drained and diced, with the rocket (arugula).

Chargrilled Pepper Salad with Pesto

The ingredients of this colourful salad are simple and few, but the overall flavour is quite intense.

Serves 4

1 large red (bell) pepper, halved
   and seeded
1 large green (bell) pepper, halved
   and seeded
250g/9oz/2¼ cups dried fusilli
   tricolore or other pasta shapes
1 handful of fresh basil leaves
1 handful of fresh coriander
   (cilantro) leaves
1 garlic clove
salt and ground black pepper

For the dressing
30ml/2 tbsp bottled pesto
juice of ½ lemon
60ml/4 tbsp extra virgin olive oil

1 Place the red and green pepper halves, skin side up, on a grill (broiler) rack and grill (broil) until the skins have blistered and are beginning to char. Transfer the peppers to a bowl, cover with crumpled kitchen paper and leave to cool slightly. When they are cool enough to handle, rub off the skins and discard.

2 Bring a large pan of lightly salted water to the boil and cook the pasta until it is *al dente*.

3 Meanwhile, whisk together the pesto, lemon juice and olive oil in a large bowl. Season to taste with salt and pepper.

4 Drain the cooked pasta well and tip it into the bowl of dressing. Toss thoroughly to mix and set aside to cool.

5 Chop the pepper flesh and add it to the pasta. Put most of the basil and coriander and all the garlic on a board and chop them. Add the herb mixture to the pasta and toss, then season to taste, if necessary, and serve, garnished with the herb leaves.

> **Cook's Tip**
> Serve the salad at room temperature or lightly chilled, whichever you like.

IRRESISTIBLE BREAD & SAVOURY BAKING

Although a huge array of different types of bread is now available from many supermarkets and bakeries, making your own is immensely satisfying and increases your choice even further. Your guests will certainly appreciate your thoughtfulness, as there can be little that is more delicious than freshly baked bread or rolls still warm from the oven.

Making bread is extremely easy and, while in many instances you have to allow time for the dough to rise, the actual preparation is not particularly time-consuming. You can mix the dough, set it aside in a warm place to rise and get on with preparing other dishes for your special meal.

The recipes in this chapter include all kinds of scrumptious breads from many different cuisines – Italian Focaccia with Green Peppercorns & Rock Salt, Jewish Challah, Syrian Onion Bread, Russian Potato Bread, and Indian Chapatis – to provide the perfect accompaniment for all styles of meal. If you really want to impress your guests, why not make decorative little rolls? There are two recipes that include detailed step-by-step instructions for shaping knots, braids, batons, spirals, and fingers for the dinner table. For those with less time available, there are plenty of delicious breads flavoured with sun-dried tomatoes, olives, cheese, herbs, spices and nuts.

This chapter also includes recipes for savoury scones (biscuits), which add the same special touch to the meal but are much quicker to make. They are especially tasty served warm and a welcome accompaniment to soups and appetizers.

Sun-dried Tomato Bread

This is one bread that absolutely everyone seems to love. Chopped onion and sun-dried tomatoes give it an excellent flavour.

Makes 4 small loaves
675g/1½ lb/6 cups strong white bread flour, plus extra for dusting
10ml/2 tsp salt
25g/1oz/2 tbsp caster (superfine) sugar
25g/1oz fresh yeast
400–475ml/14–16fl oz/ 1⅔–2 cups lukewarm milk
15ml/1 tbsp tomato purée (paste)
75g/3oz/¾ cup sun-dried tomatoes in oil, drained and chopped, plus 75ml/5 tbsp oil from the jar
75ml/5 tbsp extra virgin olive oil, plus extra for greasing
1 large onion, chopped

1 Sift the flour, salt and sugar into a large bowl and make a well in the centre. Crumble the yeast into a jug (pitcher), mix with 150ml/¼ pint/⅔ cup of the lukewarm milk and pour into the well in the flour.

2 Stir the tomato purée into the remaining milk, then add the mixture to the well in the flour, with the oil from the sun-dried tomatoes and olive oil.

3 Mix the liquid ingredients, and gradually incorporate the surrounding flour to make a dough. Knead on a lightly floured surface for about 10 minutes, then return the dough to the clean bowl, cover with lightly oiled clear film (plastic wrap) and leave to rise in a warm place for about 2 hours.

4 Knock back (punch down) the dough, and add the sun-dried tomatoes and onion. Knead until evenly distributed. Shape the dough into four rounds and place on two greased baking sheets. Cover each pair of loaves with a dishtowel and leave to rise again for about 45 minutes.

5 Preheat the oven to 190°C/375°F/Gas 5. Bake the bread for 45 minutes, or until the loaves sound hollow when you tap them underneath. Transfer to a wire rack to cool.

Warm Herb Bread

This mouthwatering Italian-style bread, flavoured with basil, rosemary, olive oil and sun-dried tomatoes, is absolutely delicious served warm with fresh salads.

Makes 3 loaves
1.3kg/3lb/12 cups strong white bread flour, plus extra for dusting
15ml/1 tbsp salt
5ml/1 tsp caster (superfine) sugar
7g/¼oz sachet easy-blend (rapid-rise) dried yeast
about 900ml/1½ pints/3¾ cups lukewarm water
75g/3oz/1½ cups sun-dried tomatoes in oil, drained and coarsely chopped
150ml/¼ pint/⅔ cup virgin olive oil, plus extra for greasing
75ml/5 tbsp chopped mixed fresh basil and rosemary

To finish
extra virgin olive oil
rosemary leaves
sea salt flakes

1 Sift the flour and salt into a bowl. Stir in the sugar and yeast. Make a well in the centre and add the water, tomatoes, oil and herbs. Beat well, gradually incorporating the surrounding flour. As the mixture becomes stiffer, bring it together with your hands. Mix to a soft but not sticky dough, adding a little extra water if needed.

2 Knead the dough on a lightly floured surface for about 10 minutes, then return it to the bowl, cover loosely with oiled clear film (plastic wrap) and leave in a warm place to rise for 30–40 minutes, or until doubled in bulk.

3 Knead the dough again until smooth and elastic, then cut it into three pieces. Shape each into an oval loaf about 18cm/7in long and place each on an oiled baking sheet. Slash the top of each loaf in a criss-cross pattern. Cover loosely and leave in a warm place for 15–20 minutes, until well risen.

4 Preheat the oven to 220°C/425°F/Gas 7. Brush the loaves with a little olive oil and sprinkle with the rosemary leaves and salt flakes. Cook for about 25 minutes, until golden brown. The bases should sound hollow when tapped.

Cheese & Courgette Cluster Bread

This unusual bread owes its moistness to grated courgettes, and its depth of flavour to freshly grated Parmesan cheese.

Makes 1 loaf
4 courgettes (zucchini), coarsely grated
675g/1½lb/6 cups strong white bread flour, plus extra for dusting
2 x 7g/ ¼oz sachets easy-blend (rapid-rise) dried yeast
50g/2oz/ ⅔ cup freshly grated Parmesan cheese
30ml/2 tbsp olive oil, plus extra for greasing
milk, to glaze
poppy seeds or sesame seeds, for sprinkling
salt and ground black pepper

1 Put the courgettes into a colander and sprinkle with salt. Stand the colander in a sink for 20 minutes to drain the juices, then rinse, drain again and pat dry with kitchen paper.

2 Sift the flour into a large bowl and add the yeast, Parmesan, 2.5ml/ ½ tsp salt and pepper to taste. Stir in the oil and courgettes, then add enough lukewarm water to make a firm but still soft dough.

3 Knead the dough for about 10 minutes, then return it to the bowl, cover with lightly oiled clear film (plastic wrap) and leave in a warm place for about 1 hour, or until doubled in bulk.

4 Lightly grease a deep 23cm/9in cake tin (pan). Knock back (punch down) the dough and knead it again. Divide it into eight pieces and roll into smooth balls. Fit these into the tin, placing one in the centre and the remainder around the outside.

5 Glaze the loaf with a little milk and sprinkle over the seeds. Cover lightly with oiled clear film and leave to rise in a warm place until the balls of dough have doubled in size.

6 Meanwhile, preheat the oven to 200°C/400°F/Gas 6. Bake the loaf for 35–45 minutes, until it is golden brown and sounds hollow when tapped on the base. Cool on a wire rack.

Spicy Millet Bread

This is a delicious spicy bread with a golden crust. Cut into wedges and serve warm with a thick soup.

Makes 1 loaf
90g/3½oz/ ½ cup millet
600g/1lb 6oz/5½ cups strong white bread flour, plus extra for dusting
10ml/2 tsp salt
7g/ ¼oz sachet easy-blend (rapid-rise) dried yeast
5ml/1 tsp caster (superfine) sugar
5ml/1 tsp dried chilli flakes (optional)
25g/1oz/2 tbsp butter
1 onion, coarsely chopped
15ml/1 tbsp cumin seeds
5ml/1 tsp ground turmeric

1 Bring 200ml/7fl oz/scant 1 cup water to the boil in a small pan. Add the millet, cover and simmer gently for 20 minutes, until the grains are soft and the water has been absorbed. Remove from the heat and leave to cool until just warm.

2 Mix the flour, salt, yeast, sugar and chilli flakes, if using, in a large bowl. Stir in the millet, then add 350ml/12fl oz/1½ cups warm water and mix to a soft dough.

3 Knead the dough on a floured surface for 10 minutes, then place it in an oiled bowl and cover with oiled clear film (plastic wrap). Leave in a warm place for 1 hour, until doubled in bulk.

4 Meanwhile, melt the butter in a heavy frying pan and cook the onion until softened. Add the cumin seeds and turmeric, and cook for 5–8 minutes more, stirring constantly, until the cumin seeds begin to pop. Set aside.

5 Knock back (punch down) the dough, knead it briefly and shape it into a round. Place the onion mixture in the middle of the dough and bring the sides over to cover it. Seal well. Place the loaf on an oiled baking sheet, seam side down, cover with oiled clear film and leave in a warm place for 45 minutes, until doubled in size. Preheat the oven to 220°C/425°F/Gas 7.

6 Bake the bread for 30 minutes, until golden. It should sound hollow when tapped underneath. Cool on a wire rack.

Olive Bread

A mixture of olives and extra virgin olive oil make this wonderful Italian bread.

Makes I loaf
oil, for greasing
275g/10oz/2½ cups strong white
 bread flour, plus extra
 for dusting
50g/2oz/½ cup wholemeal
 (whole-wheat) bread flour

7g/¼oz sachet easy-blend (rapid-
 rise) dried yeast
2.5ml/½ tsp salt
210ml/7½ fl oz/scant I cup
 lukewarm water
15ml/I tbsp extra virgin olive oil,
 plus extra for brushing
115g/4oz/I cup pitted black and
 green olives, coarsely chopped

I Lightly grease a baking sheet. Mix the flours, yeast and salt together in a large bowl and make a well in the centre. Add the water and oil to the well in the flour and mix to a soft dough. Knead on a lightly floured surface until smooth and elastic, then place in a lightly oiled bowl, cover with lightly oiled clear film (plastic wrap) and leave in a warm place to rise for I hour, until doubled in bulk.

2 Knock back (punch down) the dough on a lightly floured surface. Flatten it and sprinkle over the olives. Fold up and knead to distribute the olives. Leave to rest for 5 minutes, then shape into an oval loaf. Place on the prepared baking sheet.

3 Make six deep cuts in the top of the loaf, and gently push the sections over. Cover with lightly oiled clear film and leave in a warm place to rise for 30–45 minutes, or until doubled in size.

4 Meanwhile, preheat the oven to 200°C/400°F/Gas 6. Brush the bread with olive oil and bake for 35 minutes. Cool on a wire rack.

> **Variation**
> *Increase the proportion of wholemeal (whole-wheat) flour to make the loaf more rustic.*

Challah

With its braided shape, light texture and rich flavour, Challah is perfect for every special occasion, not just the Jewish Sabbath.

Makes I large loaf
oil, for greasing
500g/1¼lb/5 cups strong white
 bread flour, plus extra
 for dusting
10ml/2 tsp salt

20g/¾oz fresh yeast
200ml/7fl oz/scant I cup
 lukewarm water
30ml/2 tbsp caster
 (superfine) sugar
2 eggs
75g/3oz/6 tbsp butter, melted

For the topping
I egg yolk
15ml/I tbsp water
10ml/2 tsp poppy seeds

I Lightly grease a baking sheet. Sift the flour and salt into a bowl and make a well in the centre. Mix the yeast with the water and sugar; add to the well with the eggs and melted butter. Gradually mix in the flour to form a soft dough.

2 Knead on a floured surface for 10 minutes. Place in a lightly oiled bowl, cover with lightly oiled clear film (plastic wrap) and leave in a warm place for I hour, until doubled in bulk.

3 Knock back (punch down), re-cover and leave in a warm place for about I hour. Knock back, turn out on to a lightly floured surface and knead gently. Divide into four equal pieces. Roll each piece into a rope about 45cm/18in long. Line them up next to each other. Pinch the ends together at one end.

4 Starting from the right, lift the first rope over the second and the third over the fourth. Place the fourth rope between the first and second ropes. Repeat, starting from the right, and continue until plaited (braided). Tuck the ends under and place the loaf on the baking sheet. Cover with oiled clear film and leave in a warm place for 30–45 minutes, until doubled in size.

5 Preheat the oven to 200°C/400°F/Gas 6. Beat the egg yolk and water together. Gently brush the loaf with the mixture. Sprinkle with the poppy seeds and bake for 35–40 minutes.

Sweet Potato Bread with Cinnamon & Walnuts

Spicy and sweet, this tastes great both with savoury dishes and as a teabread, with cream cheese.

Makes 1 loaf
1 medium sweet potato
450g/1lb/4 cups strong white
 bread flour, plus extra
 for dusting
5ml/1 tsp ground cinnamon
5ml/1 tsp easy-blend (rapid-rise)
 dried yeast
50g/2oz/ ²⁄₃ cup walnut pieces
300ml/ ¹⁄₂ pint/1 ¹⁄₄ cups
 lukewarm milk
salt and ground black pepper
oil, for greasing

1 Bring a pan of water to the boil and cook the unpeeled sweet potato for 45 minutes, or until tender. Meanwhile, sift the flour and cinnamon into a large bowl. Stir in the dried yeast.

2 Drain the sweet potato, cool it in cold water, then peel it. Mash the flesh with a fork, then mix it into the dry ingredients with the nuts and some salt and pepper.

3 Make a well in the centre of the mixture and pour in the milk. Mix with a round-bladed knife to a rough dough, then knead on a floured surface for 5 minutes.

4 Return the dough to a bowl and cover with oiled clear film (plastic wrap). Leave in a warm place to rise for 1 hour, or until doubled in bulk. Turn the dough out and knock back (punch down) to remove any air bubbles. Knead for a few minutes.

5 Grease a 900g/2lb loaf tin (pan) lightly with oil and line the base with baking parchment. Shape the dough to fit the tin. Cover with lightly oiled clear film and leave in a warm place for 1 hour, or until doubled in size.

6 Preheat the oven to 200°C/400°F/Gas 6. Bake the loaf for 25 minutes. Turn it out and tap the base; if it sounds hollow the bread is cooked. Cool on a wire rack.

Polenta & Pepper Bread

Full of Mediterranean flavours, this satisfying, sunshine-coloured bread is best eaten while it is still warm, drizzled with a little virgin olive oil.

Makes 2 loaves
175g/6oz/scant 1 ¹⁄₂ cups polenta
5ml/1 tsp salt
350g/12oz/3 cups strong white
 bread flour, plus extra
 for dusting
5ml/1 tsp granulated sugar
7g/ ¹⁄₄ oz sachet easy-blend
 (rapid-rise) dried yeast
1 red (bell) pepper, roasted,
 peeled and diced
15ml/1 tbsp olive oil, plus extra
 for greasing
300ml/ ¹⁄₂ pint/1 ¹⁄₄ cups
 lukewarm water

1 Mix the polenta, salt, flour, sugar and yeast in a large bowl. Stir in the diced red pepper until it is evenly distributed, then make a well in the centre of the mixture. Grease two loaf tins (pans).

2 Add the warm water and the oil to the well in the dry ingredients and mix to a soft dough. Knead for 10 minutes. Place in an oiled bowl, cover with oiled clear film (plastic wrap) and leave in a warm place for 1 hour, until doubled in bulk.

3 Knock back (punch down) the dough, knead it lightly, then divide it in half. Shape each piece into an oblong and place in a tin. Cover with oiled clear film and leave to rise for 45 minutes. Preheat the oven to 220°C/425°F/Gas 7.

4 Bake for 30 minutes, until golden and the loaves sound hollow when tapped underneath. Leave in the tins for about 5 minutes, then cool on a wire rack.

Cook's Tip
Grill (broil) the (bell) pepper until blistered and beginning to char, then place in a bowl, cover with kitchen paper and set aside until cool enough to peel.

Walnut Bread

This delicious enriched wholemeal bread is filled with walnuts. It is the perfect companion for cheese and also tastes wonderful with salads.

Makes 2 loaves

oil, for greasing
50g/2oz/ ¼ cup butter
350g/12oz/3 cups wholemeal (whole-wheat) bread flour, plus extra or dusting
115g/4oz/1 cup strong white bread flour
15ml/1 tbsp light brown muscovado (molasses) sugar
7.5ml/1 ½ tsp salt
20g/¾oz fresh yeast
275ml/9fl oz/1 cup lukewarm milk
175g/6oz/1 ½ cups walnut pieces

1 Grease two baking sheets. Melt the butter in a small pan until it starts to turn brown, then set aside. Mix the flours, sugar and salt in a large bowl and make a well in the centre. Cream the yeast with half the milk. Add to the well with the remaining milk. Strain the cool butter into the well and mix with your hand, gradually incorporating the surrounding flour.

2 Knead for 6–8 minutes. Place in a lightly oiled bowl, cover with lightly oiled clear film (plastic wrap) and leave in a warm place to rise for 1 hour, or until doubled in bulk.

3 Gently knock back (punch down) the dough on a lightly floured surface. Press or roll it flat, then sprinkle over the nuts, press them in and roll up the dough. Return it to the oiled bowl, re-cover and leave, in a warm place, for 30 minutes.

4 Turn out on to a floured surface, divide in half and shape each piece into a ball. Place on the baking sheets, cover with lightly oiled clear film and leave in a warm place for 45 minutes.

5 Meanwhile, preheat the oven to 220°C/425°F/Gas 7. Using a sharp knife, slash the top of each loaf three times. Bake for about 35 minutes, or until the loaves sound hollow when tapped on the base. Cool on a wire rack.

Focaccia with Green Peppercorns & Rock Salt

There's something irresistible about a loaf of freshly baked focaccia with its dimpled surface and fabulous flavour.

Makes 1 loaf

350g/12oz/3 cups strong white bread flour, plus extra for dusting
2.5ml/ ½ tsp salt
10ml/2 tsp easy-blend (rapid-rise) dried yeast
10ml/2 tsp drained green peppercorns in brine, crushed
25ml/5 tsp fruity extra virgin olive oil
about 250ml/8fl oz/1 cup lukewarm water
20ml/4 tsp coarsely crushed rock salt, for the topping
fresh basil leaves, to garnish

1 Sift the flour and salt into a mixing bowl. Stir in the yeast and peppercorns. Make a well in the centre and add 15ml/1 tbsp of the oil with half the water. Mix, gradually incorporating the flour and adding more water to make a soft dough.

2 Knead the dough on a floured surface for 10 minutes. Return to the clean, lightly oiled bowl, cover with lightly oiled clear film (plastic wrap) and leave in a warm place until doubled in bulk.

3 Knock back (punch down) the dough and knead lightly for 2–3 minutes. Place on an oiled baking sheet and pat out to an oval. Cover with lightly oiled clear film and leave for 30 minutes.

4 Preheat the oven to 190°C/375°F/Gas 5. Make a few dimples in the surface of the dough with your fingers. Drizzle with the remaining oil and sprinkle with the salt. Bake for 25–30 minutes, until pale gold. Sprinkle with basil leaves and serve warm.

> **Cook's Tip**
> *Kneading is a vital step in bread-making as it develops the gluten in the flour. Press and stretch the dough, using the heel of your hand and turning the dough frequently.*

Dill Bread

The slightly aniseed flavour of fresh dill works well in this tasty loaf enriched with cottage cheese.

Makes 2 loaves
850g/1lb 14oz/7½ cups strong white bread flour, plus extra for dusting
20ml/4 tsp easy-blend (rapid-rise) dried yeast
30ml/2 tbsp granulated sugar
20ml/4 tsp salt
475ml/16fl oz/2 cups lukewarm water
60ml/4 tbsp light olive oil, plus extra for greasing
½ onion, chopped
large bunch of fresh dill, finely chopped
2 eggs, lightly beaten
115g/4oz/½ cup cottage cheese
milk, for glazing

1 Mix 350g/12oz/3 cups of the flour with the yeast, sugar and salt in a bowl. Make a well in the centre. Pour in the water. Beat, gradually incorporating the surrounding flour to make a smooth batter. Cover and leave in a warm place to rise for 45 minutes.

2 Meanwhile, heat 15ml/1 tbsp of the oil in a small pan. Add the onion and cook over a low heat, stirring occasionally, for 5 minutes, until soft. Set aside to cool.

3 When the onion is cool, stir it into the risen batter. Stir in the dill, eggs, cottage cheese and remaining oil, then gradually add the remaining flour until the mixture forms a dough.

4 Knead the dough on a floured surface for 10 minutes. Place in a bowl, cover with oiled clear film (plastic wrap) and leave in a warm place for 1–1½ hours, until doubled in bulk.

5 Grease a large baking sheet. Cut the dough in half and shape into two rounds. Cover again and leave to rise for 30 minutes.

6 Meanwhile, preheat the oven to 190°C/375°F/Gas 5. Score the top of each round, making a criss-cross pattern over the entire surface. Brush with the milk. Bake for about 50 minutes, until the loaves are golden brown and sound hollow when tapped on the base. Cool on wire racks.

Russian Potato Bread

Another extremely good-looking loaf, this keeps very well, thanks to the mashed potato in the dough.

Makes 1 loaf
oil, for greasing
225g/8oz potatoes, peeled and diced
350g/12oz/3 cups unbleached white bread flour
115g/4oz/1 cup wholemeal (whole-wheat) bread flour, plus extra for dusting and sprinkling
7g/¼ oz sachet easy-blend (rapid-rise) dried yeast
2.5ml/½ tsp caraway seeds, crushed
25g/1oz/2 tbsp butter
salt

1 Grease a baking sheet. Put the potatoes in a pan of salted water, bring to the boil and cook until tender. Drain, reserving 150ml/¼ pint/⅔ cup of the cooking water. Mash the potatoes and press them through a sieve into a bowl. Leave to cool.

2 Mix both types of flour in a large bowl. Add the yeast, seeds and 10ml/2tsp salt, then rub in the butter. Mix the reserved potato water and sieved potatoes together. Gradually work this mixture into the flour mixture to form a soft dough.

3 Knead on a floured surface for 8–10 minutes. Place in a lightly oiled bowl, cover with lightly oiled clear film (plastic wrap) and leave in a warm place for 1 hour, until doubled in bulk.

4 Knock back (punch down) the dough and knead it gently. Shape into an oval loaf, about 18cm/7in long. Place on the prepared baking sheet and sprinkle with wholemeal bread flour.

5 Cover the loaf with lightly oiled clear film and leave in a warm place for 30 minutes, or until doubled in size. Meanwhile, preheat the oven to 200°C/400°F/Gas 6.

6 Using a sharp knife, slash the top with 6–8 diagonal cuts to make a criss-cross effect. Bake for 30–35 minutes, or until the bread is golden and sounds hollow when tapped on the base. Cool on a wire rack.

Syrian Onion Bread

These unusual small breads come from Syria and have a spicy topping spiked with fresh mint.

Makes 8 breads
450g/1lb/4 cups strong white
    bread flour, plus extra
    for dusting
5ml/1 tsp salt
20g/³/₄oz fresh yeast
280ml/9fl oz/scant 1¼ cups
    lukewarm water
oil, for greasing

For the topping
60ml/4 tbsp finely chopped onion
5ml/1 tsp ground cumin
10ml/2 tsp ground coriander
10ml/2 tsp chopped fresh mint
30ml/2 tbsp olive oil

1 Lightly flour two baking sheets. Sift the flour and salt together into a large bowl and make a well in the centre. Cream the yeast with a little of the water, then mix in the remainder.

2 Add the yeast mixture to the well and mix to a dough. Knead on a floured surface for 8–10 minutes, until smooth and elastic. Place in an oiled bowl, cover with oiled clear film (plastic wrap) and leave in a warm place for 1 hour, until doubled in bulk.

3 Knock back (punch down) the dough and turn it out on to a floured surface. Divide into eight equal pieces and roll each into a 13–15cm/5–6in round. Make the rounds slightly concave. Prick them all over and space well apart on the baking sheets. Cover with lightly oiled clear film and leave to rise for 15–20 minutes.

4 Meanwhile, preheat the oven to 200°C/400°F/Gas 6. Mix the chopped onion, ground cumin, ground coriander and chopped mint in a bowl. Brush the breads with the olive oil, sprinkle them evenly with the spicy onion mixture and bake for 15–20 minutes. Serve the onion breads warm.

> **Cook's Tip**
> If you haven't any fresh mint, add 15ml/1 tbsp dried mint. Use the freeze-dried variety, if you can, as it has much more flavour.

Spring Onion, Chive & Ricotta Bread

Ricotta cheese and chives make moist, well-flavoured rolls or bread, both of which are excellent for serving with salads.

Makes 1 loaf or 16 rolls
15g/½oz fresh yeast
5ml/1 tsp caster (superfine) sugar
270ml/9fl oz/1⅙ cups
    lukewarm water
450g/1lb/4 cups strong white
    bread flour, plus a
    little extra
7.5ml/1½ tsp salt
1 large (US extra large)
    egg, beaten
115g/4oz/½ cup ricotta cheese
30ml/2 tbsp extra virgin olive oil,
    plus extra for greasing
1 bunch of spring onions
    (scallions), sliced
45ml/3 tbsp chopped fresh chives
15ml/1 tbsp milk
10ml/2 tsp poppy seeds
coarse sea salt

1 Using a fork, cream the fresh yeast with the sugar and then gradually stir in 120ml/4fl oz/½ cup lukewarm water. Set aside in a warm place for 10 minutes.

2 Sift the flour and salt into a warmed bowl. Make a well in the centre and pour in the yeast liquid and the remaining lukewarm water. Reserve a little of the beaten egg, then add the remainder to the liquid in the bowl. Add the ricotta and mix all the ingredients to form a dough, adding a little more flour if the mixture is very sticky.

3 Knead the dough on a floured work surface for 10 minutes, until smooth and elastic, then return it to the bowl, cover with lightly oiled clear film (plastic wrap) and set aside in a warm place for 1–2 hours, until doubled in bulk.

4 Meanwhile, heat the oil in a small pan. Add the spring onions and cook over a low heat, stirring occasionally, for 3–4 minutes, until soft but not browned. Set aside to cool.

5 Knock back (punch down) the risen dough and knead in the spring onions, with any oil remaining in the pan. Add the chives. Shape the dough into rolls, a large loaf or a braid.

6 Grease a baking sheet or loaf tin (pan) and place the bread in it. Cover with oiled clear film and leave in a warm place for about 1 hour. Preheat the oven to 200°C/400°F/Gas 6.

7 Beat the milk into the reserved beaten egg and use to glaze the rolls or loaf. Sprinkle with poppy seeds and a little coarse sea salt, then bake until golden and well risen. Rolls will need about 15 minutes and a large loaf will require 30–40 minutes. Cool on a wire rack.

> **Cook's Tip**
> To make a braid, divide the dough into three sausage-shaped pieces about 40cm/16in long. Press them together at one end and then braid, pressing the ends together to seal.

Chapatis

These chewy, unleavened breads from India are the authentic accompaniment to spicy vegetarian dishes.

Makes 6

175g/6oz/1½ cups atta or wholemeal (whole-wheat) flour, plus extra for dusting

2.5ml/ ½ tsp salt
110ml/scant 4fl oz/scant ½ cup water
5ml/1 tsp vegetable oil, plus extra for greasing
melted ghee or butter, for brushing (optional)

1 Sift the flour and salt into a bowl. Add the water and mix to a soft dough. Knead in the oil.

2 Knead on a lightly floured surface for 5–6 minutes, until smooth. Place in a lightly oiled bowl, cover with a damp dishtowel and leave to rest for 30 minutes. Turn out on to a floured surface. Divide the dough into six equal pieces. Shape each piece into a ball. Press the dough into a larger round with the palm of your hand, then roll into a 13cm/5in chapati. Stack, layered between clear film (plastic wrap), to keep moist.

3 Heat a griddle or heavy frying pan over a medium heat for a few minutes. Take one chapati, brush off any excess flour and place on the griddle. Cook for 30–60 seconds, until the top begins to bubble and white specks appear on the underside.

4 Turn the chapati over using a metal spatula and cook for 30 seconds more. Remove from the pan and keep warm, layered between a folded dishtowel, while cooking the remaining chapatis. If you like, lightly brush the chapatis with melted ghee or butter immediately after cooking. Serve warm.

Cook's Tip
Atta or ata is a very fine wholemeal (whole-wheat) flour, which is found only in Indian stores and supermarkets. It is sometimes simply labelled chapati flour.

Bagels

Bagels are great fun to make and taste wonderful with cream cheese, either on its own or with grilled aubergines or courgettes.

Makes 10

oil, for greasing
350g/12oz/3 cups strong white bread flour, plus extra for dusting
10ml/2 tsp salt
7g/ ¼ oz sachet easy-blend (rapid-rise) dried yeast

5ml/1 tsp malt extract
210ml/7½fl oz/scant 1 cup lukewarm water

For poaching
2.5 litres/4¼ pints/ 10⅔ cups water
15ml/1 tbsp malt extract

For the topping
1 egg white
10ml/2 tsp cold water
30ml/2 tbsp poppy, sesame or caraway seeds, or a mixture

1 Grease two baking sheets. Sift the flour and salt into a bowl. Stir in the yeast. Mix the malt extract and water, add to the flour and mix to a dough. Knead on a floured surface for 10 minutes. Place in a lightly oiled bowl, cover with lightly oiled clear film (plastic wrap) and leave in a warm place for about 1 hour, or until doubled in bulk.

2 Knock back (punch down), knead for 1 minute, then divide into 10 pieces. Shape into balls, cover with clear film and leave to rest for 5 minutes. Gently flatten each ball and make a hole through the centre. Place on a floured tray; re-cover and leave in a warm place, for 10–20 minutes, until the rings begin to rise.

3 Meanwhile, preheat the oven to 220°C/425°F/Gas 7. Place the water and malt extract for poaching in a large pan, bring to the boil, then reduce to a simmer. Poach two or three bagels at a time for about 1 minute. They will sink and then rise again when first added to the pan. Turn them over and poach the other side for 30 seconds. Remove and drain on a dishtowel.

4 Place five bagels on each baking sheet. Beat the egg white with the water and brush over the bagels. Sprinkle with the seeds. Bake for 25 minutes, until golden. Cool on a wire rack.

Shaped Dinner Rolls

These rolls are the perfect choice for entertaining.

Makes 12 rolls
oil, for greasing
450g/1lb/4 cups strong white
  bread flour, plus extra
  for dusting
10ml/2 tsp salt
2.5ml/ 1/2 tsp caster
  (superfine) sugar
7g/ 1/4oz sachet easy-blend (rapid-
  rise) dried yeast

50g/2oz/ 1/4 cup butter
250ml/8fl oz/1 cup
  lukewarm milk
1 egg, beaten

For the topping
1 egg yolk
15ml/1 tbsp water
poppy seeds and sesame seeds,
  for sprinkling

1 Grease two baking sheets. Sift the flour and salt into a bowl. Stir in the sugar and yeast. Rub in the butter. Add the milk and egg and mix to a dough. Knead on a lightly floured surface for 10 minutes. Place in an oiled bowl, cover with oiled clear film (plastic wrap) and leave in a warm place for 1 hour.

2 Knock back (punch down) the dough on a floured surface and knead for 3 minutes. Divide into 12 pieces and shape.
Braid: divide the dough into three sausages. Pinch together at one end, braid, then pinch the ends and tuck under.
Trefoil: make three balls from a piece of dough and fit them together in a triangular shape.
Baton: shape a piece of dough into an oblong. Slash the surface.
Cottage roll: divide a piece of dough into two-thirds and one-third and shape into two rounds. Place the small one on top of the large one and make a hole through the centre.
Knot: shape a piece of dough into a rope and tie a single knot.

3 Place the rolls on the baking sheets, cover with oiled clear film and leave in a warm place for 30 minutes, until doubled in bulk. Meanwhile, preheat the oven to 220°C/425°F/Gas 7.

4 Mix the egg yolk and water and brush the rolls. Sprinkle with poppy seeds and sesame seeds. Bake for 15–18 minutes.

Panini All'olio

The Italians adore elaborately shaped rolls.

Makes 16
60ml/4 tbsp extra virgin olive
  oil, plus extra for greasing
  and brushing

450g/1lb/4 cups strong white
  bread flour, plus extra
  for dusting
10ml/2 tsp salt
15g/ 1/2 oz fresh yeast
250ml/8fl oz/1 cup
  lukewarm water

1 Lightly oil three baking sheets. Sift the flour and salt into a bowl. Cream the yeast with half of the water, then stir in the remainder. Add to the flour with the oil and mix to a dough.

2 Knead the dough on a floured surface for 8–10 minutes. Place in a lightly oiled bowl, cover with lightly oiled clear film (plastic wrap) and leave in a warm place for about 1 hour, or until the dough has nearly doubled in bulk.

3 Knock back (punch down) on a lightly floured surface. Divide into 12 equal pieces and shape into rolls as described below.

4 Tavalli (twisted spirals): roll each piece of dough into a strip about 30cm/12in long and 4cm/1 1/2in wide. Twist each strip into a loose spiral and join the ends of dough in a circle.
Filoncini (finger-shaped rolls): flatten each piece of dough into an oval and roll to about 23cm/9in long. Make it 5cm/2in wide at one end and 10cm/4in wide at the other. Roll up from the wider end, then stretch to 20–23cm/8–9in long. Cut in half.
Carciofi (artichoke-shaped rolls): shape each piece of dough into a ball.

5 Place the rolls on the baking sheets. Brush with olive oil, cover with oiled clear film and leave in a warm place for 30 minutes. Preheat the oven to 200°C/400°F/Gas 6.

6 To finish the carciofi, snip four or five 5mm/1/4in deep cuts in a circle on the top of each ball, then make five larger horizontal cuts around the sides. Bake the rolls for about 15 minutes. Cool on a wire rack.

Cheese & Potato Scones

The addition of mashed potato gives these moist scones a crisp crust.

Makes 9

40g/1½oz/3 tbsp butter, plus extra for greasing
115g/4oz/1 cup wholemeal (whole-wheat) flour, plus extra for dusting
2.5ml/½ tsp salt
20ml/4 tsp baking powder
2 eggs, beaten
60ml/4 tbsp semi-skimmed (low-fat) milk
115g/4oz/1⅓ cups cooked, mashed potato
45ml/3 tbsp chopped fresh sage
50g/2oz/½ cup grated mature Cheddar cheese
sesame seeds, for sprinkling

1 Preheat the oven to 220°C/425°F/Gas 7. Grease a baking sheet. Sift the flour, salt and baking powder into a bowl. Rub in the butter, then mix in half the eggs and all the milk. Add the potato, sage and half the Cheddar and mix to a soft dough.

2 Knead the dough lightly on a floured surface until smooth. Roll it out to 2cm/¾in thick, then stamp out nine scones (biscuits) using a 6cm/2½in fluted cutter.

3 Place the scones on the prepared baking sheet and brush the tops with the remaining beaten egg. Sprinkle the rest of the cheese and the sesame seeds on top and bake for 15 minutes, until golden. Cool on a wire rack.

> **Cook's Tip**
> Use a sharp cutter to avoid compressing the edges of the scones (biscuits), which would prevent them from rising evenly.

> **Variations**
> • Use unbleached self-raising flour (self-rising) instead of wholemeal (whole-wheat) flour and baking powder, if you like.
> • Fresh rosemary or basil can be used in place of the sage.

Caramelized Onion & Walnut Scones

These are good buttered and served with mature (sharp) cheese. They are also excellent with soup.

Makes 10–12

90g/3½oz/7 tbsp butter
15ml/1 tbsp olive oil
1 large onion, chopped
2.5ml/½ tsp cumin seeds, lightly crushed, plus a few extra
200g/7oz/1⅔ cups self-raising (self-rising) flour, plus extra
5ml/1 tsp baking powder
25g/1oz/¼ cup oatmeal
5ml/1 tsp light muscovado (molasses) sugar
90g/3½oz/scant 1 cup chopped walnuts
5ml/1 tsp chopped fresh thyme
120–150ml/4–5fl oz/½–⅔ cup buttermilk or smetana
a little milk
salt and ground black pepper
coarse sea salt

1 Melt 15g/½oz/1 tbsp of the butter with the oil in a small pan and cook the onion over a low heat, covered, until softened but not browned. Uncover, then continue to cook gently until it begins to brown.

2 Add the crushed cumin seeds and increase the temperature slightly. Cook, stirring occasionally, until the onion browns and begins to caramelize around the edges. Cool. Preheat the oven to 200°C/400°F/Gas 6.

3 Sift the flour and baking powder into a large bowl and add the oatmeal, 2.5ml/½ tsp salt, a generous grinding of black pepper and the muscovado sugar. Rub in the remaining butter, then add the onion, walnuts and thyme. Stir in enough of the buttermilk or smetana to make a soft dough.

4 Roll or pat out the mixture to just over 1cm/½in thick and stamp out 5–6cm/2–2½in round scones (biscuits). Place on a floured baking sheet, brush with milk and sprinkle with a little coarse sea salt and a few extra cumin seeds. Bake for 12–15 minutes, until well-risen and golden brown. Cool the scones briefly on a wire rack and serve warm.